FREEDOM TO ROAM

D0305430

HOWARD HILL

Freedom to Roam

THE STRUGGLE FOR ACCESS TO BRITAIN'S MOORS AND MOUNTAINS

Moorland Publishing

British Library Cataloguing in Publication Data

Hill, Howard
    Freedom to roam.
    1. Outdoor recreation - Great Britain - History
    2. Trespass - Great Britain - History
    I. Title
    333   GV191.48.G7

    ISBN 0-903485-77-X

ISBN 0 903485 77 X

Photoset by Advertiser
Printers Ltd, Newton Abbot
and printed in Great Britain by
Redwood Burn Ltd,
Trowbridge & Esher for
Moorland Publishing Co Ltd,
PO Box 2, 9-11 Station Street,
Ashbourne, Derbyshire,
DE6 1DZ.

Contents

List of Illustrations

Preface

A short while ago, a northern newspaper carried a report of landowners'
reactions to the suggestion that there should be a right of access on foot to all
common land in the North Pennines. Much of this land is used for sheep
grazing and shooting and a land agent was quoted as saying;

> Any interference by the public with the management of these grouse moors
> would mean a substantial loss of income not just for the owners but for hundreds
> of beaters, gamekeepers and so on. It could seriously injure the whole rural
> economy in the Durham uplands.

This preposterous but revealing remark shows how little attitudes have
changed in some quarters. The evidence that little or no damage is done to
sheep and grouse as a result of allowing access on foot is now clear, and is
referred to in this book. Moreover, the economies of some rural areas have
undoubtedly *benefitted* from their popularity with ramblers. For example,
if walkers and climbers were suddenly barred from the Lakeland fells their
cries of protest would probably be matched by those of hoteliers and
publicans horrified at the prospect of losing so much custom!

However, it is too much to hope that the mindless and prejudiced opposition to public access will disappear overnight. As Howard Hill shows,
it has persisted since at least the Industrial Revolution. Insofar as this
opposition has been overcome in some areas, it has taken time, money and,
occasionally, militant action to do so. This book chronicles the battles that
have been fought and the notable, albeit limited successes that have been
achieved by the outdoor movement. It has involved a 150-year campaign
for what citizens of most European countries take for granted — a right of
access to mountain, moorland and other uncultivated land.

There is still much to work for. In the first place, although *de facto* access
exists over much of upland Britain, it is nevertheless often challenged.
In the last year or so, The Ramblers' Association has been concerned with
restrictions on access in the Forest of Bowland, in the Arans and the Nantlle
Ridge of North Wales, and in the deer forests of the Scottish Highlands.
These restrictions are likely to grow in number and extent. It is therefore
vital that we secure a *statutory* right of access to such open country before
disputes, in areas where *de facto* access exists at the moment, become more
widespread. Fortunately, there are signs that a statutory right of access to all
common land — perhaps a million and a quarter acres in all — will be

established within the next few years, and this will be an important step on the way to the wider legislation that we are looking for.

Second, we must press for more access to woodland and waterside areas. Here, the access agreement machinery — with its provisions for compensation and wardening — is much more appropriate than it is in the uplands. There are indications that farmers and landowners would actually *welcome* more access agreements for such areas, but sadly local authorities and successive Ministers have been unwilling to use their powers to make such agreements. Nor has the Countryside Commission done much to encourage them, preferring instead to use its financial resources for country parks, picnic sites and urban fringe management schemes. These are certainly to be welcomed, but the Commission's neglect of access agreements for woodland and riverbank shows an imbalance in its priorities for which it can be justly criticised.

Third, a long hard look needs to be taken at legislation on rights of way and long distance paths. To a large extent, this legislation has failed, and failed miserably. In theory, the law prohibits the obstruction and ploughing up without restoration of footpaths and bridleways. In practice, these statutes are honoured more in the breach than in the observance. In theory, local authorities have a duty to protect the rights of the public and to signpost public paths. In practice, they disregard these duties with impunity. In theory, legislation allows for the creation of long-distance paths free of motor traffic. In practice, these routes have taken decades to establish, the Countryside Commission is not taking any more schemes on board, and trail riders still roar along the Ridgeway. Farmers naturally think that rights of way legislation is deficient from their point of view as well, and the time has come for both sides jointly to examine the statutes and to see if ways cannot be found of breaking out of the deadlock that has existed now for far too long.

Fourth, we should never become complacent about past achievements. One of the starting points in this book is the campaign to save Epping Forest — a campaign which culminated in the declaration by Queen Victoria in 1882 that the Forest would henceforth be open to the public without let or hindrance. Yet the centenary of that declaration may coincide with the mutilation by the Department of Transport of the southern end of the Forest — they want land for a new dual carriageway road to link the M11 with the Blackwall Tunnel. Open space gained in the past can never be regarded as being wholly secure.

Howard Hill touches on most of these themes and he concludes that, in order to meet the challenge of the future, 'it is now time for the open-air organisations to draw closer together.' He is quite right. We are fragmented and isolated and are in no position to use to the full the political influence of the millions of outdoor enthusiasts in this country. Newcomers to the movement often ask, for example, why the Ramblers' Association and the Common, Open Spaces and Footpaths Preservation Society continue to exist as separate entities; and why such co-ordinating committees as do exist (for example the Council for National Parks and the Outdoor Pursuits Division of the Central Council for Physical Recreation) are not a lot stronger. The answer probably is that the open-air movement suffers from a good deal of institutional inertia which will not be broken down unless a powerful new initiative is launched. Such an initiative will certainly be needed if we are to cast off the image of the 1930s and capture the imagination of a generation of outdoor enthusiasts who know little and care less about the access campaigns of the past.

Howard Hill's book will help to re-awaken interest in the history of the outdoor movement, and his account is a fascinating one. He is bound to be criticised for injecting his own opinions and for not seeking to hide his political leanings, but this is all to the good as it makes his work easily readable and highly provocative.

Alan Mattingly
The Ramblers' Association

Introduction

The Open Air Movement has become a major social phenomenon of many industrialised countries during the twentieth century. Having started as a mere trickle around the middle of the nineteenth century, it now embraces millions of ordinary people, many of whom have joined together into organisations catering for the varying needs of their outdoor activities. Forecasts of future trends project an even more rapid growth. The House of Lords Select Committee Report on Sport and Leisure, based upon surveys commissioned by the Post Office, estimated that by the end of the century demand for recreational facilities will rise by one-fifth, this being one consequence of an 8 per cent reduction of working hours per man. With a 13 per cent expected growth in the population on top of this, it is obvious that by the end of the century leisure demands will have become among the most urgent of social problems.

Judging by the experience of the USA, the major part of the demand will be concentrated in the countryside, the coast, or areas of water, rather than the urban sports field. A pilot National Recreational Study by Keele University (British Travel Association, 1969) found that 12 per cent of all those active in outdoor recreation were ramblers and hill walkers, exceeded only by fishing (14 per cent).

A similar statement was made in the Report of the National Parks Policies Review Committee (the Sandford Report) which claimed that the demand for hill walking, climbing, camping and nature study was likely to double by the end of the century. The statement also pointed out that once interest is aroused in these forms of outdoor activity, unlike many other forms of physical recreation, it tends to persist throughout a person's life.

The demand for leisure ranks high in the scale of Human Rights. If food, shelter and clothing are primary requirements, relaxation and leisure are what life is about. Yet to obtain the happy satisfying life which is the dream of all people, the demands of both these requirements must be closely interrelated. The open-air movement was a result of the industrialisation of the nineteenth century when there was a desire to walk the moors and dales of rural Britain and climb its mountains, especially where this could be done close to the growing industrial towns of the Midlands, the North, and the Metropolis. Today the movement is nationwide, embracing all centres of population and covering a wide variety of activities: sailing, golf, fishing, bird-watching, etc. A day in the country, usually in the family car, is among the most popular of all attractions.

Much concern has been expressed on the problem of conservation, ecology, the spread of urbanisation and how to meet the growing leisure needs of the British people. There has been surprisingly little written on the history of the open-air movement, particularly rambling; this book attempts to remedy this omission. The experience gained in the past hundred years will provide a sound basis for the examination of the future leisure needs of the British people.

1 Escape from the Industrial towns

The rise and growth of the popular open-air movement has been attributed to the nineteenth and twentieth century revolt against urban existence. Today 90 per cent of the people of Britain live in towns; in the middle of the last century the proportion was about half; a hundred years earlier, less than a quarter.

This is how it was put in the Footpaths and Access to the Countryside Report in 1947:

> Fostered by the instincts of an urbanised population, torn increasingly from its ancient roots in the soil by the industrial revolution, an urban existence that pushes the primeval background out of sight, that makes it remote and unavailable, that deprives people of intimate contact with it . . . is unlikely to produce adequate men and women.

The towns of Shakespeare's day were little more than overgrown villages, though rapidly increasing in size and wealth, and they were more insanitary than the villages. Nevertheless, they were still rural and agricultural communities as well as centres of industry and commerce. Defoe, in his *Tour of the Whole Island of Great Britain* (1724-5) found Manchester '. . . the greatest mere village in England'. During his time it was a noted centre of manufacture, which had begun earlier than the great woollen manufacturers in other parts of England. He described the West Riding of Yorkshire as wealthy and 'most populous', having 'the greatest manufacturers, and consequently the greatest share of the wealth'. It seems that the thing which impressed him about Sheffield was the narrow streets and the 'houses dark and black occasioned by the continued smoke of the forges.' He found the town of Halifax as healthy as any other part of England, with 'these people all full of business', which was the clothing trade. He was so impressed by the presence of coal below the ground and running water from the hills that he thought it had been 'directed by the wise hand of Providence.'[1]

The Industrial Revolution wrought a dramatic change in this. Small country towns, never far from the open country, serving straggling industrial villages, were transformed by a process of expansion into the great conurbations of the late nineteenth century, from which the workmen found it 'harder and harder to escape out of the wide web of smoke and squalor that enveloped their daily life', as G. M. Trevelyan wrote in his book *English Social History*. For the workman, Manchester was a prison. 'From this foul drain the greatest stream of human industry flows out to fertilize the whole world. From this filthy sewer pure gold flows. Here humanity attains its most complete development and its most brutish, here civilization works its miracles and civilised man is turned almost into a savage.'[2]

'The charming green valleys of the Ribble, the Irwell, the Mersey and their tributaries — a country which a hundred years ago was chiefly swamp land thinly populated, is now sown with towns and villages and is the most densely populated strip of country in England.'[3] The Manchester of Defoe's day had been transformed into one of the worst of the industrialised towns with 'dense overcrowding in cellar dwellings of unspeakable filth.'[4] Other boom towns were equally bad. Charles Reade said of a Sheffield suburb in *Put Yourself in his Place* (1891):

> Though built on one of the loveliest sites in England, it is perhaps the most hideous town in creation. All ups and downs and black slums . . . and bristles with high round chimneys. . . . They defy the law, and belch forth massy volumes of black smoke, that hang like acres of crepe over the place, and veil the sun and the blue sky even in the brightest day . . .

Yet the Industrial Revolution did much more than create 'industrial cities of squalor and ugliness unequalled in Europe'. It created a work force the likes of which Britain had never seen before:

> The English Spinner Slave has no enjoyment of the open atmosphere and breezes of heaven. Locked up in factories eight stories high, he has no relaxation until the ponderous engine stops and then he goes home to get refreshed for the next day. No time for sweet association with his family; they are all alike fatigued and exhausted.
> *Black Dwarf*, 30 Sept 1818[5]

It was in these 'dark Satanic Mills' which are dotted all over the landscape of South Lancashire and West Yorkshire that men, women and children, as Robert Owen observed, were being transformed 'into virtually a new kind of human being'.[3] Rigid disciplines were enforced: play, singing, even talking were stamped out. The time allowed to answer the calls of nature were strictly rationed. The rigid disciplines degraded labourers and made them 'less than men'.[7] It reduced men to machines which 'Ends not infrequently in becoming an intellectual one himself, employed in continually increasing what it is impossible for him to enjoy.'[8]

Little wonder that Keats when he first saw Windermere said that it made him forget the divisions of life — the discord and the suffering. The view he saw produced a harmony, as it did for other pastoral poets who, escaping from the strife and struggles of the hideous towns, saw the countryside as their last refuge.

Wordsworth has been described as the doyen of the Lake Poets, 'the poet of nature in all her moods', and it is also said of him that he was the inspiration of the open-air movement, who by starting the art of fell walking set the tone of the ramblers' movement.

Wordsworth is credited with being the first to have had the vision of preserving the natural beauty of the Lakes for posterity. 'A part of national property in which every man has a right interest who has an eye to perceive and a heart to enjoy.'

But, as G.M. Trevelyan in *The Call and Claims of Natural Beauty* notes, 'to some early men, even late eighteenth century mountains were a forbidding, harsh and desolate region.' That was what Dr Johnson thought of the Isle of Skye and Defoe of the Peak. As Trevelyan shows, the intellectuals came for esoteric reasons. 'Nature', he writes, 'can fortify and console even in southern woodlands . . . but to many the moorlands and mountains seem to have more rugged power and faithfulness with which in solitude we can converse.'

Yet it was the hands manning the factories, digging the coal, the pen pushers working in cramped ill-lit offices who grasped the reality of the world. They came not to gain fresh vigour from which the more effectively to pursue their 'thirst for gold' to quote Wordsworth. Nor to make a new religiosity from the scenery as did so many eighteenth and nineteenth century writers, but to recapture the humanity which they had lost in the factories and mines of the industrial revolution.

'Why is it', asked Henry Salt in his *Cumbrians and Cumbrian Hills*, 'that we find a humanising influence even in the wastes where our grandfathers could see nothing but what repelled them as savage and ferocious?' The answer was supplied by the more perceptive poets and writers, but above all by the working-class ramblers. As Carlyle observed: 'men are grown mechanical in head and heart as well as hand'. So to gain freedoms from the antagonisms of the workplace they went to the countryside, not to look at nature with the dreaming gaze of poets but to regain good fellowship, amidst the mountains and dales, away from the antagonistic relationship of the factory. As the *Sheffield Clarion Handbook* put it, 'The joy of walking, . . . and the pleasure of companionship, are amongst nature's best gifts to man.'[9]

Unlike the literary figures of the eighteenth and nineteenth centuries, the working class could neither desert the towns to live in the countryside nor spend weeks walking through it. But that does not mean they needed or appreciated it any the less. The reason, as Dr Kay remarked to the Public Works Committee in 1833, was that there were 'few hours between labour and sleep'.

'Thousands of men and women left the rapidly growing squalor of the industrial towns in an effort to find healthful exercise in the open air.' The Manchester MP Richard Potter (grandfather of Beatrice Webb) stated: 'Vast numbers of people passed in the early morning by my house to the Race Course on Sundays, particularly in the spring and summer . . . I might say thousands every week.' They also 'went into the fields to play football even though there was no place reserved', stated an MP for Bolton. In Liverpool Dr Lyon Playfair stated: '. . . 20,000 persons passed over the river to Cheshire on Sunday to enjoy their walk. . . .'[10]

The reason for this exodus to the countryside was as Dr Kay of Manchester said: 'All scenes of interest are remote from the town . . . During the last fifty years from the increase of building and augmented value of property many open spaces have been enclosed and every day the increasing multitude become more and more restricted in their means of reaching any healthy place to walk in.' One such place in Sheffield had been the Park, a considerable part of which was built on in the early nineteenth century. 'Most bitterly have many artisans expressed themselves . . . on their virtual exclusion from participating in the outdoor recreation of the other classes.'[11] Yet many Sheffield workpeople 'walked miles on Sundays to reach the open moors'.[12] The MP Joseph Brotherton said that 'several pretty walks in Salford twenty or thirty years ago . . . are now closed or built upon' with the result that, as Dr Kay said 'the walks which can be enjoyed by the poor man are chiefly the turnpike roads, alternatively dusty and muddy.' But the working people went and trespassed. The MP for Bradford complained that ' . . . considerable trespass is done across the fields by so large a population.'

In fact one of the reasons given by the Leeds MP for providing public walks and open spaces for the humbler classes was that it would prevent trespass. It would also 'keep them from the low and debasing pleasures of the public house and the drinking shops', of which a Hampshire magistrate said in 1833 that it was not altogether the beer but the fellowship to which he objected.

Limited though their hours away from the factory were, the people were eager to escape from the towns. Mrs Gaskell wrote in *Mary Barton* (1848): 'There are a class of men in Manchester and all the manufacturing districts of Lancashire who know the name and habitat of every plant within a day's walk from their dwellings.' In fact the more venturesome spirits would steal a holiday of a day or two when any particular plant was in flower, for the purpose of fetching it home. Some just went out into fields and woods at meal times to 'listen to the song of summer birds or watch the trembling waters of the Luddon. . . .'[13]

These men and women were the forerunners of those who formed the rambling clubs.

References to Chapter 1

1 Defoe, Daniel, *A Tour through the Whole Island of Great Britain* (3rd edition 1742, Penguin English Library 1971), p492

2 de Tocqueville, Alexis, *Journeys to England and Ireland*, as quoted in E.J. Hobsbawm, *The Age of Revolution* (1962), p24

3 Engels, F, *The Condition of the Working Class in England* (1844), Panther edn p75

4 Thompson, E.P., *The Making of the English Working Class* (1968 ed), p355

5 *Ibid*, p220

6 Williams, R., *Culture and Society 1780-1950* (1967), p26

7 Ruskin, John, quoted in Williams, *op cit*, p142

8 Southey, Robert, quoted in Williams *op cit*, p23

9 *Sheffield Clarion Ramblers*, 1920-21. (This series of booklets is often referred to as the *Clarion Handbook*, and will subsequently be cited under that name).

10 Playfair, Dr L., *Commission of Inquiry into the State of Large Towns and Populous Districts* (1845), Part II, Appendix, p31

11 Symon, J.C., *Report in the Trades of Sheffield and the Moral and Physical Condition of Young Persons Employed in Them* (1843), p8

12 Pollard, S., *A History of Labour in Sheffield* (1959), p28

13 Thomson, *op cit*, p324

2 The Clubs and the Early Struggles

The Gentlemen's Clubs The earliest rambling clubs were not drawn from a wide stratum of British people. They were what have been called 'Gentlemen's Clubs' whose members came from the ranks of the well-to-do: the legal, literary, and political circles of Victorian Britain. Closely associated with them in time were the early climbing and mountaineering clubs, many of which combined fell walking with rock climbing.

Yet for all their eminence, some of them had just as much trouble with the shooting gentry as did their counterparts drawn from the humbler classes. One such club was the London-based Sunday Tramps, formed by Leslie Stephen on November 2nd 1879, and numbering among its supporters George Trevelyan and George Meredith. It had a number of off-shoots, at least one in Canada and another in Edinburgh. Their first rambles started from Stephen's house in Wimbledon. Later he introduced the idea of taking a train to some country railway station, walking twenty or more miles and returning by another station. *The Times,* on 18 January 1930, gave an account of a celebration dinner held on the occasion of the club's fiftieth anniversary. It reported how in order to avoid the high roads, they discreetly trespassed on the game preserves of the aristocracy. This brought them into conflict with the gamekeepers, and they had a novel way of rebuffing them. In unison they would repeat after the leader in solemn chant this carefully devised legal formula:

> We hereby give you notice that we do not, nor doth any of us, claim any right of way or other easement into or over these lands and we tender you this shilling by way of amends.

'The effect on the gamekeeper', commented *The Times,* must have been devastating.' Whether or not this is so, there is no doubt of the reception which awaited the northern ramblers walking on the grouse moors of the Peak, or the deer forests of Scotland. They were chased off by gamekeepers, armed with thick sticks, dogs, and sometimes guns.

At least two similar clubs were formed in Yorkshire: the Sheffield-based Derbyshire Pennine Club, whose members were drawn from the ranks of leading industrialists, and the Yorkshire Rambling Club formed in 1899 in Leeds. The latter was at pains to dissociate itself from any controversies which might have led to litigation and for this reason disaffiliated itself from the Commons Preservation Society, which had been formed in 1865 by a group of radical Whigs to preserve what remained of the London common lands.

From the earliest times to the present day no issue has aroused a longer history of struggle than has the uses and ownership of land. Before the urbanized people of England were seeking 'air and exercise' commoners had been fighting a losing battle to retain their rights in the land against the private enclosers.

1 Epping Forest, Essex, the scene of nineteenth-century struggles against the enclosers.

At the time of the first enclosures sanctioned by Parliament in 1235 it was estimated by Lord Eversley in his book *Commons Forests and Footpaths* (1910) that ' . . . two-thirds of [the land in] England was, at that time Commons or Waste land of Manors. . . .' W.G. Hoskins joint author with L. Dudley Stamp, of *The Common Lands of England and Wales* (1963) states that though 'One cannot estimate, even roughly, how much land in England and Wales was common land at the time of the Norman Conquest, . . . it amounted to several million acres there can be no doubt.' Since the Black Death a losing battle had been fought to retain the commons. By the 1870s no more than between one-and-half and two million acres were left.

From time immemorial commoners have exercised their right to turn out their cattle and sheep for pasture, and to dig turf, cut gorse, bracken and heather for fuel, litter or thatching, on common land. Though generally the public have not unlimited rights of access locally there may be rights of 'air and exercise', especially according to Lord Eversley 'In the more mountainous parts of England and Wales the common rights over wide ranges of land have been the means of securing to the public the unrestricted access to and enjoyment of mountain tops, and have prevented the owners of land from excluding the public. . . .' Of importance to this book is Hoskin's statement 'Not all the wild, uncultivated lands of England and Wales were common land, however. Much was pure "waste", of no use to anyone . . .' and for most part they were 'dreary uplands'.

Around 1860 a movement began in London to stop the Lords of the Manor selling what was left of the commons to speculative builders. This was more than an effort to retain a footpath, which is about the public's right of passage over tracks. It was the forerunner of the later struggles, for the right of access to all uncultivated land, which is the main topic of this book.

The battle for the London Commons has often been presented as mainly one which was fought out in the Courts and Parliament by a number of public spirited men and women, such as John Stuart Mill, Sir William Harcourt, Lord Eversley, Miss Octavia Hill, and by James Bryce, who formed the Commons and Open Spaces Preservation Society in 1865. While not wishing to detract in any way from the role they or the society played, it is well to remember that the more important part was played by the nameless thousands of people who took direct action to halt the enclosures.

Lord Eversley in his book *Common Forests and Footpaths* states quite clearly that it was the protest against the savage treatment meted out to three labourers arrested and jailed for lopping trees in Epping Forest that was largely responsible for its being saved. He records how, on 10 November 1879, five to six thousand people turned out to exercise their right to lop trees following the enclosers' three-year refusal to obey a Court injunction to remove the fences they had erected twenty years earlier. This action eventually compelled them to yield back three thousand acres of land. Queen Victoria on 11 May 1882 declared the forest open to the public without 'let or hindrance'.

Epping Forest has always been considered as of major importance. Its origins are lost in antiquity, but by 1793 it consisted of 9,000 acres of open land

2   The Forest Ramblers Club was formed in 1884 to retain Epping Forest as an open space.

and was much used by the public for recreation. But by 1848 it had been reduced to 7,000 acres. In 1884 the Forest Ramblers' Club was formed by some London businessmen. The name 'Forest' indicates the objectives of this club — to walk 'through Epping Forest and report obstruction we have seen'. Members scorned the company of ladies on their walks: 'membership is still exclusively male although twice a year the club condescends to invite ladies on coach outings.'

A club having similar radical tendencies was formed in Scotland in 1889, known as the Cairngorms Club, with James Bryce as its first President. Before its actual formation the founder members had already experienced many encounters with stalkers, ghillies and lairds during expeditions across the high Cairngorms. This was a direct result of the rapid extension of the deer forests and the change from shooting grouse 'over the dogs' to 'driving'. As a consequence, old drovers' roads and coffin roads had been closed, inns and hostelries shut down.

Dr E.A. Baker in his book *The Highlands with Rope and Rucksack* (1923), said that

The aim of owners of deer forsts is to create a huge solitude first by removing such human population, then closing mountains and glens to the public. They

21

have succeeded in doing this throughout a large portion of ten counties; of 543 peaks obtaining the Munro Standard 3000 feet above sea level, nearer 500 than 400 are situated in this forbidden land.

Dr Baker added that inns and hotels had been closed to keep out the holidaymakers of small means. He reported how the finest walk in the British Isles via Glen Affric and through Glen Lichd was no longer possible since the closure of the Shiel Inn and other hostelries, which were robbed of their licences.

In 1845 the Rights-of-Way Society was formed with the purpose of stopping such illegal closures of footpaths. On learning of a closure the society's members would challenge it by erecting previously prepared signposts declaring the track to be an ancient right-of-way. This society has many victories to its credit including Jock's Road in Glen Doll; but the most famous was 'Battle of Glen Tilt'. John Hutton Balfour, Professor of Botany at Edinburgh University, set out in 1847 with seven of his students to collect

3   *The scene of the 'Battle of Glen Tilt', in Perthshire, which took place in 1847.*

botanical specimens. He was unaware of the opposition the party was likely to encounter from the truculent sixth Duke of Atholl. On an earlier expedition he had experienced a brush with the Earl of Fife's keepers when climbing Ben MacDhui, by the forbidden Luibeg route. On this occasion he was met by the Duke of Atholl's ghillies, whence ensued a protracted argument which was only ended by the botanical party scrambling over a wall, thus circumventing the opposition. Enormous publicity was generated, leading to a protracted lawsuit, conducted on behalf of the Edinburgh Assocation for the Protection of Public Rights of Roadways in Scotland, which was finally decided by the House of Lords in the Association's favour. This established a vital precedent.

Not all the Scots were so radically motivated. Professor Ramsay, President of the Scottish Mountaineering Club — formed one year after the Cairngorm Club — specifically dissociated the club from what he called 'stravaging' or 'marauding' activites. 'I and my friends have no desire to see the proposed club mixed up with any attempt to form rights of way.'[1] The club's constitution laid down the following principle: 'The members of the club shall respect proprietary and sporting rights and endeavour to obtain the co-operation of the proprietors.' This was later used in the 1930s by the then Duke of Atholl in his opposition to the Access to Mountains Bill.

This in no way inhibited James Bryce and his radical friends from following up the successes against the closure of the London commons. In 1884 Bryce, who was MP for South Aberdeen, took the struggle into Parliament when he proposed a bill which would have granted the right of access to all uncultivated mountains and moorlands in Scotland. The issue which sparked it off was the now famous MacCrae case, which was only indirectly connected with public access. An American millionaire, W.L. Winans, had acquired 200,000 acres of land in Kintail for use as a deer forest. It was guarded by an army of sentinels. One of MacCrae's children allowed his pet lamb to stray upon Winan's unfenced land whereupon Winans sought an interdict, which the court granted. The effect of this ruling was to prevent any recurrence, but on hearing the decision MacCrae slaughtered all his animals including the lamb. This aroused widespread anger, which according to Baker reached fever heat and a petition protesting against Winan's behaviour was signed by many people of all classes.

The 1884 bill did not pass through Parliament, but it was followed by a number of similar proposed bills in the early years of the twentieth century, which would have extended the principle of right of access to uncultivated land in England and Wales. Only twice during this period did a proposed measure make any progress through the House of Commons. The first time was in 1892 when the House approved the principle of the measure, and again in 1908 when Annan Bryce, James' brother, presented a bill along with another moved by C.P. Trevelyan relating to England and Wales. Both bills were referred to the Standing Committee of the House.

The most remarkable feature of the debates on these two bills was the support received from all three major political parties. The Liberals, who formed the Government of the day, viewed the measure sympathetically; the

Tory spokesman said that his party was deeply committed to the measure; while Ramsay Macdonald spoke strongly in its favour and stated he had himself trespassed in many of the forbidden deer forests of Scotland. Churchill and Macdonald, both future Prime Ministers, voted for the bill. But another forty years were to pass before a bill that in any way compared with all these proposals was finally put on the Statute Book; even then as we shall see, it was different in many respects from what Bryce and Trevelyan had sponsored.

The People's Rambling Clubs By the last quarter of the nineteenth century, in all parts of urban Britain, especially the industrial towns, the people's rambling movement was emerging, and gradually they began to take over the leadership of the struggle for access. The major reason for this was the growing popularity of the Swiss mountains which, being completely free to walk and climb on, drew the gentlemen ramblers and climbers away from Britain. The Alps, said Leslie Stephen, were 'places of refuge where we may escape from ourselves and our neighbours'.[3] He called them the 'Playground of Europe', in a book of that title written in 1871. As early as 1840 there were 3,000 visitors to Chamonix, most of them English. Few, if any, were members of the people's rambling clubs. Tied as they were to the industrial machine, workers had neither the time nor the money to roam at will through the magnificent valleys or to climb the awe inspiring mountains of Switzerland.

Scotland was the birthplace of many early rambling clubs whose members were drawn from the ranks of the ordinary people. The *Glasgow Herald*, 26 December 1892, carried a report of a well-attended public conference convened under 'the auspices of the recently formed West of Scotland Ramblers' Alliance'. It must have been the first of its kind in Britain and was made up of ten rambling clubs, all based in the Glasgow area. Its purpose was to discuss 'the advantages of rambling as a means of recreation and education'. Most of the participants named in the report were parsons. The rambling clubs represented were those which were linked to the YMCA and the United Presbyterian Churches. For this reason they confined their rambles to Saturday afternoons, as did the rambling clubs formed in 1896 by the Men's Meeting and Literary Assocations of Edinburgh West End Mission. The Chairman of the 1892 conference outlined the purpose of the rambles, which was to study the geology, biology and botany of Glasgow and its neighbourhood. Unlike the Forest Ramblers, the chairman expressed pleasure at the presence of 'Lady members as well as male'; this he said would ensure the social side being 'carried to its utmost capacity'.

At this period there were quite a number of other rambling clubs formed in Scotland. Four of these are worthy of mention. They are the Dundee Club formed in 1896, the Ramblers Round Glasgow in 1869, the Sylvan Ramblers in 1885, and the Old Printers' Devils in 1870; the last named had its counterpart in Edinburgh and its name reveals quite clearly its social composition. Both the Old Printers' Devils and the Sylvan Ramblers must have experienced some difficulties on their rambles, for they took the precaution of acquiring permits before starting out. Hazards even more severe had faced their rambling predecessors. 'A band of functionaries termed "Compurgators" were employed to perambulate the streets and walks during "Kirk hours" on Sunday, in order to compel "Stravaigers" either to go to church or to take themselves to their homes. Those who refused compliance were at once taken into custody.'[4]

Nor were footpath battles unknown. The most famous was the battle of 'Harvie's Dykes'. One Thomas Harvie erected a wall blocking a footpath along the banks of the Clyde in 1823. The enraged Glaswegians' smashed it down with pickaxes and crowbars. A party of dragoons was despatched to arrest the ringleaders, who were sent to gaol.[5]

According to the Liverpool Ramblers' Federation Handbook (1927) the earliest rambling club to be started in that city was the YMCA, formally established in 1874, though day excursions had been part of the YMCA's activities from its inauguration in 1846. Membership was at firstly strictly a male preserve, though later they relaxed this male exclusiveness and allowed lady friends to join in alternate rambles. For some inexplicable reason they dropped their male chauvinism completely 'after a visit to a lunatic asylum'.

The Liverpool Hobnailers was another club that started around the 1890s. Their name gives a clue to their gear. While they wore ordinary suits their boots were hob-nailed, which in these days of moulded rubber soles are virtually unknown. They were really tough ramblers who used to go out with the intention of walking in areas where access was restricted, such as on some of the hills around Llangollen.

The presence of women on rambling excursions did on occasion cause problems with Victorian morality, and maybe it was this which led to the formation of a women's only climbing club named the Pinnacle Club, which had a hut below Snowdon where members occasionally invited the men in for coffee. The women members of the Midland Institute of Ramblers, formed in 1894 by the student teachers at the Birmingham and Midland Institute of Adult Education, had a piece of string attached to their long skirts so that they could be hitched up when getting over stiles or walking through mud and yet appear 'respectable' when walking on roads. More serious for them, however, was the 'No Road' sign which they once encountered on a public footpath running by the side of Yardley Church — 'A deception by which some landowners seek to deprive the public of the few lingering rights over their Native Land which they still retain.' Up to the 1940s this club also had a rule that the cost of the monthly rambles should not exceed 2s 6d.

The Federation of Rambling Clubs was formed in 1905 with about a dozen clubs. It was solely a London creation and was later to become the Southern Area of the Ramblers' Association. The jubilee issue of its Handbook explained that the federation was an offshoot of the Commons, Open Spaces and Footpaths Preservation Society. When it started it was certainly the only federation of ramblers' clubs in the country, and has always had the distinction of being the largest of the regional organisations which comprise the variously named ramblers' organisations.

Getting to and from the towns into the countryside has always been among the most elementary needs of urban-dwelling ramblers. This was before the motor-car age; the main transport available up to 1912 was the railways; wages were low, and the London Federation appears to have been notably successful in negotiating cheap railway fares for travelling out to one countryside station and returning from another. Between the years 1893 and 1910, one of the most famous of all London ramblers, E.S.Taylor — who used the pseudonym 'Walker Miles' — compiled a series of rambles covering the counties of Kent, Surrey and North London, which linked all the railway stations in a given area. They were regularly published under the title 'The Field Path Rambles'. One of the earliest triumphs of the London Federation, recorded in the jubilee number of its Handbook, was in concluding an arrangement with the Great Northern Railway Company which granted concessionary fares for the sole use of constituent rambling clubs. The early issues of the *London Ramblers' Handbook* read like a ramblers' *Bradshaw*. Refreshments at reasonable prices were no less important. Included in every issue was the catering list, giving the locations of cafes and pubs that welcomed ramblers.

These are the bread-and-butter problems of every country seeker from the much publicized Everest expeditions with their Sherpas and camps, to the more humble strolls along the Downs of southern England, the deer forests of Scotland with their mountain bothies, or the bleak uplands of the now famous Pennine Way. So it is not surprising that one of the priorities of all rambling clubs whatever their location, has been the provision of cheap transport and refreshment.

Lancashire and Yorkshire Clubs   The rambling clubs which were to spearhead the fifty years' struggle for access to mountains were formed in the industrial north — Lancashire and Yorkshire. Their members came from the opposite end of the social spectrum to that of the Gentlemen's Clubs. They drew together a goodly sprinkling of men and women from the early Trade Union, Co-operative and Labour movements. Lewis Paton in his introduction to T.A.Leonard's *Adventures in Holiday Making* recalls that Blatchford's *Merry England* was just out, and socialism was bound to be the bone of contention 'which in the open air could be discussed without coming to blows or thinking the other fellow a fool'. G.H.B.Ward, the founder of the Sheffield Clarion Club, records how 'the few who responded to our call to ramble were for the most part the studious mechanic or clerk'. The principles upon which the clubs were founded were directly linked with the social system of the society in which they lived: they aimed not only to get away from the noise, grime and filth of the industrial towns of the North, but also from the 'money grubbing outlook', to quote T.A.Leonard, who has been christened the father of the open-air movement.

In 1893 Leonard formed the Co-operative Holidays Association, which since its inception has been greatly influenced by the ideals of the co-operative movement. It had its birth in the bleak upland township of Colne in north-east Lancashire. The inhabitants of this region were mostly 'hard working millfolk', and when the wakes week came round each year there was a general exodus to Blackpool and Morecambe, which led to thoughtless spending of money and inane types of amusement. The formation of a rambling club was part of the social guild work of a Congregational Church of which T.A.Leonard was minister. 'We planned a Guild Holiday at Ambleside June 1891 when over thirty young men spent Saturday scaling Wansfell and Helvellyn.' From this was formed the Co-operative Holidays Association — a non-profit-making organisation which, to emphasise this, rejected the use of the word Limited. Unlike some of the earlier rambling clubs drawn from whichever part of the social scale, they welcomed women into their ranks.

4 *The Co-operative Holiday Association's centre at Keld, Swaledale, in 1899, where men and women shared holidays.*

The Co-operative Holidays Association was one of the first movements to offer young Victorians of both sexes opportunities outside of churches and chapels for meeting each other on a footing of equality and goodwill. 'In the very early days this caused some to have grave misgivings and it is interesting to recall that at one time it was seriously questioned [by outsiders] whether it were wise to allow womenfolk to share the holiday.' In addition the servants at the holiday centres were treated almost as guests. They considered 'the old servant system' as 'part of the bad social system that we were determined to get rid of.' In 1913 Leonard started the Holiday Fellowship out of the Co-operative Holidays Association because he felt the first very successful

5 *Servants were treated as guests at the Co-operative Holiday Association's centre.*

venture was not quite fulfilling the ideals upon which he founded it. 'We were not making the progress in international work we had hoped for.... We felt also that despite our working-class origins we were becoming rather middle-class in spirit and conservative in ideas.... We want to bring holidays within the reach of the poorer folk.... '[7]

To return to the main fight for access to the mountains, it was ramblers of Manchester and Sheffield who formed the hard core of the struggle which has won, within the Peak, the legal right of access to 56 per cent of its grouse moors. This is not surprising, for there is no part of Britain so distinctively situated. It covers an area of over 200 square miles, surrounded by the industrial conurbations of Lancashire, Yorkshire, Nottinghamshire, Derbyshire and Staffordshire. Half of the population of England lives within 60 miles of its borders, and it is visited by over 15 million people every year. The scenery is one of striking contrasts, stretching from the Dove which flows through the loveliest dale in England — Cowper's 'Sweet stream, that winds through yonder glade' — in the south, to the bleak, and in these days alluring, uplands of Kinder Scout and Bleaklow to the north.

By the middle of the nineteenth century in almost every town and village of Lancashire and Yorkshire botanical societies were established to study the area's natural history, especially the local flora. With only the rarest exceptions the men which these societies attracted were self-educated manual workers, mostly textile operatives with a sprinkling of craftsmen from other trades. 'These men lived for the most part in grinding poverty, but they explored the area more thoroughly than any comparable area has ever been explored. . . .' One of the earliest societies was formed in Eccles, then a village near Manchester, as early as 1777. District associations were formed and at the great annual meetings as many as 200 would attend. It was not unusual for these working-class naturalists to ramble thirty miles a day to enjoy '. . . the beauties of nature with as much zest as I ever did in my life', to quote Richard Buxton, a 62-year-old clog maker. Buxton never earned more than fifteen shillings a week, and 'had the greatest difficulties in procuring the necessaries of life.'[8]

Phil Daley, an official of the Manchester Ramblers' Federation for over 35 years, says that it is claimed that the Manchester YMCA Rambling Club is one of the oldest in the country, dating its birth around the 1880s. It had a reputation for undertaking very strenuous walks; between Saturday afternoon and Sunday evening they would walk seventy miles over the moorlands. The Manchester Rambling Club was formed in 1907. 'Macs

6 *Members of the Manchester Rambling Club after an all-night walk in 1909.*

Ramblers' were named after two of the pioneers — Macauley and McMurdo. One of these Macs has described how 'Thirty years ago [ie 1918], organised ramblers in the Manchester area were content to limit their co-operation to the support of the local footpath society', which has a record of organised struggle stretching back almost 150 years.

Harold Wild, another figure prominent in the Manchester rambling movement, has traced the pioneering history of the footpath societies in Manchester. The first committee in that city to organise resistance to footpath closure was set up in 1826 to oppose the action of a landowner who, to give his estate a more park-like appearance, began removing footpaths and fences. Having succeeded on his own land he attempted to do likewise on adjacent property. In this he was aided by two brother magistrates who signed the necessary diversion orders. Before the orders were confirmed by Quarter Session, the local people took a hand in the matter, breaking down the obstructions and restoring the original path by treading down his oats. Harold Wild recounts many similar local incidents. The committee known as the Manchester Association for the Preservation of Ancient Footpaths on a number of occasions took direct action against the unlawful closures.[9] 'Five members of the committee together with a workman carrying suitable tools . . . wrenched a barrier down and levelled the banking.' The committee's reputation acquired national status. Soon other parts of the country, facing landowners closing ancient rights-of-way, were seeking the aid of the Manchester Committee in their own battles. Harold Wild records that help was sought from Preston, from Boston Spa and North Allerton in North Yorkshire, and from Hull, Sheffield, and Derby. In these last two places there were societies which were offshoots of the Manchester Committee. They were the Hallamshire Footpath Preservation Society and the Derbyshire Footpath Preservation Society. Two official authorities, Chorlton Union at Chorlton-on-Medlock and the Worksop Board of Health, wrote letters in 1860 and 1865 respectively seeking help in countering threatened encroachments at Wentworth by Lord Fitzwilliam and by the Duke of Portland, who was promoting a parliamentary bill to divert five miles of the Worksop and Mansfield turnpike road from passing through his estate. Yet the strangest plea for help came from the West Riding Prison at Wakefield, which sought information about how to open an old footpath which had been stopped up; it is not clear whether it was the prisoners or the governor who enquired. In 1824 an Association for the Protection of Ancient Footpaths was also set up in York.

The most historic of all early northern footpath struggles which the Manchester Committee helped to win, was the twenty-year fight waged by the people of Hayfield in the Peak District to reopen the William Clough path leading from the village of Hayfield, along William Clough, under Kinder Scout, to the Snake Inn on the Sheffield to Manchester road. It had from time out of mind been freely used as a bridle path linking the Hayfield valley and the fertile Woodlands Valley. It was closed by the Duke of Devonshire, whose grouse moors it crossed, because it interfered with the grouse shooting of his tenant, a mill owner. This track was used by, among others, the followers of

John Wesley who were numerous in the villages of Hayfield, Edale and Bradwell, to travel to their annual 'Love Feast' which was, and still is, held in a barn in Alport Woodlands in the heart of the Peak. This 'Feast of Charity' was an occasion when the rich made contributions to feed the poor. During the first three centuries of the Christian era it was held in the churches; then, owing to criticism by unbelievers, it was discontinued, but revived by the Moravians in the seventeenth century and adapted by the Wesleyans, who had quite a big following in this part of the Peak. According to the *Methodist Recorder,* 10 April 1908, 'So highly did the Duke of Devonshire appreciate the religious work of his tenants in the Woodlands, that his grace in 1866 built a pretty little chapel which stands in a field by the roadside some 2½ miles below the Snake Inn.' This however did not prevent the Duke along with two other landowners from closing the path ten years later. The result was a vigorous twenty-year struggle; during this long period £1,000 was raised to finance the fight, which was conducted by the Hayfield and Kinder Scout Ancient Footpaths Association and continued by the Northern Counties and Peak District Preservation Society.[10] The battle was eventually won and the village celebrated the victory with great pomp, a brass band playing at the dedication ceremony.

The Northern Counties Footpaths Preservation Society has many more victories to its credit, as any rambler can see in the shape of the cast-iron footpath signs which it has erected on many moorland tracks in the Peak.

Sheffield Clarion Ramblers   One of the most remarkable of all the early clubs was the Sheffield Clarion — a name used by early socialists at the turn of the century. It combined in a way that no other club appears to have done, the

7   G.H.B. Ward pointing out landmarks to the early Clarion Ramblers.

need to re-establish the sense of fellowship between men amid the objects of nature. This aim quickly brought it into conflict with the powerful vested land interests pursuing their hunting and game shooting privileges which were so widely extended following the Norman Conquest.

The club has been described by its founder and guardian spirit for 58 years — the redoubtable G.H.B. Ward — as the 'first Sunday workers' rambling club in the north of England'.[10] In the *Clarion Handbook* for 1921-2 he writes:

> The Club was born on the first Sunday in September 1900. Kinder Scout footpath was opened during the previous year, [Ward made a mistake here — it had been reopened in 1897] it occurred to me that others might wish to accompany me, and I advertised in the *Clarion* [an early socialist weekly edited by Robert Blatchford]. The day was fine and clear, and fourteen attended [eleven men and three women].... En route it was decided that I should organise some rambles during 1901 and we had five monthly walks....During 1901 it was decided that we must have an official existence and a Committee was formed.

A Labour councillor was elected president. Sheffield's first Labour MP, Mr Joe Pointer, became president in 1910. The first official booklet (entitled *Sheffield Clarion Ramblers*) was issued in 1902 and comprised a four-page card with routes of nine summer rambles, about a hundred words of annotation, and one poem.[11] Prominently printed on the front cover were the words 'The Rambler who doth own the bond of fellowship.' In 1906 this was replaced by Ward's phrase 'A rambler made is a man improved.' This has remained its motto throughout the remainder of its sixty-three issues, with the exception of 1910.

Ward was no solitary who 'loathing the stern reality of rush and push, the din and devilry of city strife'[12] wanted to turn back the wheel of history to a Golden Age which never existed. Even when he sat alone on Margery Hill in the heart of his beloved Peakland, surrounded by vast expanses of the heather clad moors and valleys, he was thinking of a life that ought to be. It was this which made him a Socialist, the first secretary of the Sheffield Labour Representation Committee; and unlike many of the Romantic poets of earlier times he went into the countryside not to forget about the horrors of the city, but to help himself and his associates — the working men and women of Sheffield — to regain some of their lost humanity. Seldom when confronted by big landowners did he shirk a fight, especially when by enclosing the moors and mountains and the fertile valleys, they made it difficult to realise Ward's simple creed, 'A rambler made is a man improved.'

Writing in the *Clarion Handbook* of 1934-5, he explains how

> Rambling is also a culture and a craft . . . an intense love for one's own country, the innermost and the most remote parts of it, the sweetest as well as the wildest, a love for the wind and the rain, the snow and the frost, the hill and the vale, the widest open spaces and the choicest pastoral and arboreal retreats. It is a love for valley and moorsides, their history and their lore, which cannot be exhausted, a love which . . . compels a devotion and adoration which is equal to some men's religion.

8 G.H.B. Ward, who founded the Clarion Ramblers in 1900, seen in 1953
during the search on Howden Moors for a missing 86-year-old shepherd.

Few people had more knowledge of the history of the Peak than had the Clarion Ramblers. Ward spent thousands of hours searching through the old records, unearthing all the details of the enclosures, the ancient tracks, the origins of the guide stones used by the early travellers, the early struggles of Peakland dwellers. He insisted that other members of the club should become equally knowledgeable. The 1921-2 booklet sets out the duties of Ramble Leaders, which are still relevant today. These are the main ones: the ramble will be taken wet or fine; the leader *must* follow the printed route; he has full charge of the arrangements for the day, and is expected to write in advance and make some provision for tea; he is expected to provide a reading, or to give useful information upon the way (place names etc) from ramblers' booklets or other sources, and to see that some song is sung during the day.

Responding to a question 'Is Club Rambling worth while?' Ward replied: 'It never was to those who don't like that sort of thing or those superior persons who have no desire to associate with their fellows.' Yet 'lifelong pleasure and benefit' has been given 'to some thousands of our fellows who, first learning from a club or walking in a pack or crowd, soon discovered that more intense pleasure came from a walk with a few boon companions.' And again, ramblers would 'Never become ramblers in the true sense of the word' without the existence of a popular rambling club. 'Hundreds of old members since 1900 can testify to the truth of this assertion.'[13]

The early ramblers were often frowned on by the puritanical sabbatarians, who preached an abstemious and hard-working moral life in this world, in exchange for eternal salvation in the next. The passport to this happiness was to be a three-times attendance at church on Sundays. Yet Sunday was the only complete day in which to enjoy companionship among the charms of nature.

It was in 1897 that the break came for Ward, a Sunday school teacher, when he was turned out of his local church by the vicar. Thus, he said, the church played a part in forming the first working-class Sunday rambling club. T.A. Leonard, himself a minister, had to face similar religious intolerance when he formed the Co-operative Holidays Association in 1891.

No sooner were the ramblers of Manchester and Sheffield roaming over the tops of the peat moors, than they were chased off by the gamekeepers of the grouse-shooting owners. For decades battles had been in progress against those who were intent on closing the ancient footpaths and bridleways. Long prior to the advent of the turnpike road, these tracks, many dating from before Anglo-Saxon times, had become established rights of way between the earliest communities.

Since the first appearance of private land ownership, battles had to be fought to maintain these rights of way. The earliest footpath preservationists were the country folk. With the advent of the industrial towns it was the urban dweller who became their foremost protectors. These struggles were reflected in the evidence given to the Select Committee on Public Walks. Richard Potter MP was a leading member of this committee, and declared that they had 'been effective in preventing the closure of many footpaths which would otherwise have been stopped to the public.' The committee's reputation became so effective as to stop landlords in the town of Bury, where there was no committee, from closing footpaths.

Yet important as was the preservation of these ancient tracks, it was not enough. Some of the most inviting uplands, such as the Kinder Scout plateau and Bleaklow, had no right of way over them. Yet these were the very areas 'affording in many ways the most exhilarating and picturesque scenery'[14] in the district. This particular comment applied to Kinder Scout, an area of fifteen square miles of mountainous country with no public path.

Phil Barnes, who in his early days was a well known Sheffield rambler, printed in his booklet published in 1934 a map of the Peak surrounded by the towns of South Lancashire, and West and South Yorkshire, showing the rights of way. He commented:

> Although Bleaklow is only sixteen miles in a straight line from the centres of Manchester and Sheffield, there are, surrounding this ridge, thirty-seven square miles of wild country, quite unknown except to a few ramblers who defy the unjust restrictions and take the access so far denied them by law. Similarly to the east of the Derwent reservoirs there are the extensive Broomhead, Howden and Derwent moorlands, in all covering thirty-two square miles, with only three undisputed public ways across them. . . . Throughout the moorland area in and adjacent to the Peak District (about 215 square miles) there are as a matter of fact only twelve footpaths across moorland which exceed two miles in length.'[15]

Barnes also produced a report in 1934 for the Sheffield Council for the preservation of rural England detailing the ownership of the grouse moors to which access in Derbyshire was refused. There were seventeen private owners, made up of three dukes, one earl, two knights, two army officers, eight industrialists, and one local authority.

The struggle for the right to wander freely over these vast expanses of uncultivated moorland was not to establish a new freedom but to regain an old one. This particularly applied to the moorlands of the Peak, for as Dr E.A. Baker writes in his article 'The Forbidden Lands':

> Kinder Scout, Bleaklow Head, the Langsett, Saddleworth and Yorkshire moors were a different case. These barren tracts never had the abundance of pasture where the commoner could graze his beasts, or of woods and spinneys where he had the right to gather fireing; hence the claims to commonage were unimportant. Thus the moorlands remained *waste lands* out and out and nobody troubled much about them. So far as access to them was concerned, no let or hindrance was interposed by needless landowners.[16]

Thus the reason given to justify the enclosure of grazing and cultivated land — to increasing food production — applied less, if at all, to much of the moorland uplands. But this did not save them from being taken into private ownership, either by being enclosed or being given away following the dissolution of the monasteries and the break-up of the Peak Forest. Ward lists in the *Clarion Handbook* 153½ square miles of moorland enclosed, with a further ten to twenty thousand acres given away to the various big landowners such as the Eyres, Devonshires, Norfolks and Shrewsburys.[17]

As for Kinder Scout, this was not enclosed until 1836. Ward quoted a statement made by William Walker to the Manchester Literary Club on 22 March 1880 which reads 'This Kinder Enclosure Act (1836) and its award of 2000 acres S.W. and W. outliers of Kinder Scout'.[18] A statement in the booklet *Kinder Scout* (published in 1880 by the Hayfield and Kinder Scout Ancient Footpaths Association) declares:

> A great part of Kinder Scout and the adjoining moors were until lately what is known as 'King's Land', over which the public might ramble at their pleasure; but about the year 1830 the whole of these lands were surveyed, and allotted to the various owners of contiguous lands, according to the size of their holdings.[19]

The right to 'ramble at pleasure' over Kinder Scout is confirmed in the statement of the *Manchester Geographical Society Journal* 1897: 'Thirty or forty years ago the Scout was a happy hunting ground for us who were then young. . . .'[20] Not so for the Manchester and Sheffield ramblers. Kinder Scout became known as the 'forbidden mountain', to quote from an article by Edwin Royce, the editor of the *Manchester Ramblers' Handbook,* and one of the most forthright champions in the access to mountains campaign. He wrote: 'No sacred mountain in Tibet is more strictly guarded. It must not be walked upon without permission given in writing; it must not be photographed without permission of the owner; even to print its name may be an infringement of his rights.'[21] To the modern Kinder Scout walker striding out on the Pennine Way this may seem an exaggeration, but it was no exaggeration to those who ventured into the area during the first forty years of this century.

Doctor's Gate   The earliest recorded struggle in which the Sheffield Clarion Ramblers were involved was the battle to reopen the ancient right of way known as Doctor's Gate. Before the opening of the Snake turnpike road in 1821, this track was the only way from Glossop on the west side of the Pennines to Woodlands and Ashopton on the east side, traversing some of the wildest and most hazardous parts of the Peak.[22] The track near the summit has an overall width of 10ft — 6ft of road and with two 2ft ditches. It was built by the Romans around AD78, for use by the Frisian Legion in subduing the rebellious natives of the Peak,[23] and is a truly remarkable piece of road engineering. To traverse it on horseback was not without its risks; one traveller records that ten years before parliament authorized the building of the turnpike road in 1818, 'one false step would bring destruction to the rider and horse.'

Shortly after the opening of the new turnpike road Lord Howard, the owner of the land across which the path goes, closed Doctor's Gate, so as to preserve the privacy of his grouse moor. Unfortunately for him he had no legal right to do this, for no legal application was ever made to the Commissioners to stop travellers from using the old track, so that its use by local people and those unable to pay the tolls continued.

In October 1898 the Peak District and Northern Counties Footpath

9   *The Clarion Ramblers uncovering the Roman road, Doctor's Gate, in the early 1900s.*

10   *One of the 'joint raids' on Doctor's Gate in 1909 by ramblers from Sheffield and Manchester.*

Preservation Society opened negotiations with Lord Howard to have the obstruction removed. These negotiations dragged on for 'ten fruitless years', to quote Ward. It was then that the rambling clubs of Manchester and Sheffield took a hand. G.H.B. Ward claims that the Clarion Ramblers were the first to walk the full length of the ancient track during 1909, which they did in single file, and after that the Manchester Ramblers walked defiantly over it for five years. More important is his statement of 'Three joint raids by the Clarion and Manchester Ramblers in 1909-11', which received publicity, and in 1911 an amicable settlement was reached. The land-owner agreed to open the path and repair some portion of it and the society, while not admitting to any limitation of public use of the path at all times, nevertheless asked ramblers to refrain from using it during the breeding and shooting season. Lord Howard however, had the gate at the Mossylee (Glossop) end of the path wired up, which the society considered was a repudiation of the agreement.

From August 1912 the Clarion Ramblers organised a special annual ramble over Doctor's Gate until 1920, designating their excursions as

11   A demonstration at the Mossylee end of Doctor's Gate in 1910. Note the 'No Road' sign.

Celebration Rambles during which they walked the whole way. On 5 September 1920 they walked over its entire length with the Manchester Ramblers Mac Club, and the next year they were reinforced by the Holiday Fellowship Salford PSA, to be followed a year later by further reinforcements from Barnsley and Glossop. On 15 September 1927 the Manchester Federation organised a two way assault on the disputed track. One of the parties, according to *Out of Doors* 15 September 1927, was 100 strong. On one of these occasions G.H.B. Ward smashed the padlock on the Mossylee Gate. Eventually the right of way was re-established on a slightly altered route. The Derbyshire County Council authorized the re-erection by the Peak District and Northern Counties Footpath Preservation Society of two notice boards.

The Sheffield Clarion Ramblers gave birth to dozens of other clubs in Sheffield. One such club was characteristically named the Onward, formed by members of the Clarion who claimed that other members dallied too long over their midday Sunday pint and sandwiches. The influence of the Sheffield Clarion also extended into many other towns and cities of Britain, some adopting the name Clarion. One, named the Tyneside Sunday Ramblers, was formed in 1919 using as its motto Ward's words 'The man who never was lost never went very far.'

The Lake District Before the heather-clad moorlands of the Peak attracted the first trickle of working-class ramblers, tourists had been flocking to the Lakes, encouraged by the pastoral poetry of Wordsworth. The earliest influx of tourists were 'the moneyed intellectuals, the professors, the retired clergymen, the not-quite-so-retired business men.'[24] In their footsteps followed the ramblers drawn from the northern industrial towns. There were no abusive gamekeepers waiting to drive them from the fells, such as they had to face in the Peak, for nowhere among the wide variety of wild life found in the 1,000 square miles of Lakeland were there any red grouse. These, as we shall see later, were the reasons for the northern ramblers being excluded from the Peak.

Although the Lakeland hills provided grazing for thousands of sheep the presence of many walkers and climbers, even in lambing times, causes no real problems. The foxes — for this is John Peel country — are a far greater menace. Nevertheless there were access problems, the most serious being the attempt by Manchester Corporation to prevent tourists walking on their water gathering grounds. The original bill for Haweswater sought to extinguish the right of access to 22½ square miles of common land because it was water gathering ground. Employees and tenants of Wythburn and South Thirlmere were not allowed to accommodate overnight visitors, and were even forbidden to provide refreshments. These were the days which preceded the introduction of modern filtration techniques. Nevertheless, the Commons Preservation Society was successful in securing some limitations to these restrictions. The most famous was included in the Birmingham Corporation Act of 1892 which became known as the Birmingham Clauses.

The Lake District did not completely escape the long drawn out attempts by landowners to obliterate footpaths, probably the most famous being the one in which Wordsworth was involved. The *Manchester Guardian*, 7 October 1887, recounts how Wordsworth was once journeying to Lowther Castle to attend a dinner in his honour, at which the Lord Chief Justice and Mr Justice Coleridge were to be present. They passed down Patterdale by Ullswater, then, leaving the chaise, they struck across some fields towards the castle. Suddenly the path ended in a blind wall. The poet muttered something and attacked the wall as if it were a living enemy, crying out, 'This is the way, an ancient right of way too', and passed on. That evening after the ladies had left the room, Mr Justice Coleridge said to Sir John Wallace who was a near resident: 'Sir John, I fear we committed trespass today; we came over a broken-down wall on your Estate'. Sir John seemed irate and said that if he could have caught the man who broke it down, he would have horsewhipped him. The grave old bard at the end of the table heard the words, the fire flashed into his face and rising to his feet he answered: 'I broke your wall down, Sir John, it was obstructing an ancient right of way, and I will do it again. I am a Tory, but scratch me on the back deep enough and you will find the Whig in me yet'.

12   *Hindscath in the Lake District, where there were footpath battles.*

According to an article in the *Contemporary Review* of 1886, no less than twenty-two supposed rights of way had been closed against the tourist, and it was the closure of the footpath through Fawe Park, and over Latrigg, which gave rise to the formation of the Keswick and District Footpath Preservation Association in 1856.[25] The would-be footpath closers were a Mr J.J. Spedding and Mrs Spencer Bell, who in addition to abusing the Footpath Society caused to be erected:

Huge barriers of iron and wood . . .and saturated it with coal tar to stop an organised protest walk over the path in dispute. . . . On Wednesday, September 28 between four and five hundred people went to Fawe Park and on Saturday October 1st about two thousand people walked to the top of Latrigg. These have been disrespectfully called a mob of loafers, whereas they were as respectable, as orderly, as well dressed, and as fine a body of people as could be brought together in any part of Her Majesty's dominions. Amongst these so-called loafers were to be found Ministers of religion, doctors of long-established reputation, solicitors, a Member of the House of Commons, ladies and gentlemen. . . . Never did a crowd of people meet more as a family and more exemplify that there is a groundwork of goodness at the bottom of all human nature. The people of Keswick who were present at Fawe Park and Latrigg are fighting the battle of all lovers of this beautiful district, this garden and playground of England . . . the Latrigg case will affect the right of ascent to almost every mountain in Great Britain.[26]

References to Chapter 2

1 Aitken, R., 'Stravagers and Marauders', *Scottish Mountaineering Journal*, Vol. 30 (1975), p351
2 Rossiter, J.P., *An Analytical Study of the Public Use of Private Land for Outdoor Recreation in England, 1949-1968* (Unpublished PhD thesis, Dept of Land Economy, University of Cambridge, 1972), p18
3 Pimlott, J.A.R., *The Englishman's Holiday: A Social History* (Hassocks, Sussex 1976), p201
4 MacDonald, H., *Rambles Round Glasgow* (Glasgow, 1854), p20
5 Ibid, p32
6 Leonard, T.A., *Adventures in Holiday Making* (Guernsey, 1934), p14
7 Ibid, p53
8 Stephenson, T., 'Footpath Stoppers and Early Ramblers', *Rucksack, Journal of the Ramblers' Association*, Spring 1977 and Summer 1977
9 Wild, H., 'The Manchester Association for the Preservation of Ancient Footpaths', *The Manchester Review*, 1965-6, p242
10 *Clarion Handbook*, 1950-1
11 Ibid, 1921-2
12 Ibid, 1907
13 Ibid, 1930-1
14 Barnes, P.A. *Trespassers Will Be Prosecuted* (Sheffield, 1934), p5
15 Ibid, p5
16 *Ramblers' Federation Handbook* (The official year book of the Ramblers' Federation, Manchester and District), 1924

17 *Clarion Handbook*, 1941-2
18 Ibid, 1941-2
19 *Kinder Scout. The Footpaths and Bridle Roads about Hayfield* (1880)
20 *Ramblers' Federation Handbook*, 1923
21 Ibid, 1938
22 Ibid, 1923
23 *Clarion Handbook*, 1913-14

24 Nicholson, N., *The Lakers: The Adventures of the First Tourists* (1955), p112
25 Rawnsley, E.F., *Canon Rawnsley— An Account of his Life* (Glasgow, 1923)
26 Letter published in the *Manchester Guardian* 7 October 1887

3　The Grouse and the Deer

What was it that turned the apparently useless 'wastes' into such valuable preserves as to warrant the violent evictions, lasting for over half a century, of the city ramblers from the peakland uplands? Rev H.A. Macpherson in *The Grouse — Natural History* published in 1894 supplies the answer: 'It is hardly too much to say that the red grouse enjoys a unique position among the members of the feathered community.' The grouse is indigenous to Great Britain and Ireland, but only to certain regions. It will not thrive except on the heather moors of Scotland, Northern England, Wales and Ireland, as it feeds mainly on the tips of *Callunus Vulgaris*. Efforts have been made to rear it on the royal estates at Sandringham, and also in the Lake District; Count Kniphausen attempted to introduce it into Germany. All to no avail.

According to Professor J.T. Coppock, 'There are thought to be 4.5 to 5 million acres of grouse moors, but grouse are shot over a much wider range of the country.' 'A good grouse moor', he continues, 'is more valuable for sport than for agriculture and on one 100,000 acre estate the sporting rent was approximately two-tenths per acre and the agricultural one-quarter.'[1] He does add that generally sporting rents are much lower.

An article in the *Scottish Field* — a hunting, shooting and fishing journal — gives an account of the history of the grouse:

> Unlike other creatures which have been hunted, trapped and shot from the earliest times, grouse didn't appear on the social scene until the fifteenth century when the Scots Parliament enacted that wild fowl 'fit for the sustenance of man' were to be preserved. . . .By the sixteenth century the bird was declared to be very delicate eating, and an almost immediate result was that its shooting was for a time legally prohibited. All concerned with grouse were slow to recognise that a gold mine was being neglected. Even the keenest sportsmen failed to understand what was really waiting for them. The poacher promptly took to wild fowl and was long a thorn in the side of the sovereign laird and Parliament, but his depredations were mainly caused by the general poverty of the country. . . .The prices obtained in the south were very considerable. The year 1800 particularly marks the changing condition of sport, especially with grouse. It could neither be bought nor sold and was an exclusive attribute to the landlord class and their personal friends.[2]

A letter published in the *Gentleman's Magazine* boldly stated that 'God himself, is the creator of all things, [and] gave man a right to kill and eat the birds of the air, [and] the beast of the field'[3] and the Romans defined this right very precisely. The right of ownership belonged to whoever could reduce wild animals to possession. The enclosures later took vast tracts of land into private ownership, strictly delineated by walls and hedges, and in the process extinguished any common rights in the soil, which also applied to all game found on the privately owned land. This is the reason why Kinder Scout, Bleaklow and all the other out-and-out waste lands of the Peak District were enclosed in the eighteenth century.

13   Grouse shooting from the butts in Perthshire. In the background there are miles of open moorland to which legal access is denied for the rambler.

Malcolm and Maxwell in *Grouse and Grouse Moors* attribute to Rimington Wilson of Broomhead Hall in the Peak District the distinction of being the first to shoot grouse on the wing, at the turn of the eighteenth and nineteenth centuries. There was also grouse shooting in Scotland at around this time in Perthshire and Inverness and in the Lowlands and Border Counties. However, unlike the Yorkshire and Derbyshire moors the Scottish ones did not have the advantage of being near the metropolis.

There were three other factors which contributed to the tense situation which faced the Manchester and Sheffield ramblers at the end of the nineteenth century. Up to the middle of the century the method of shooting grouse and pheasants was 'over the dogs', when one or two shooters would follow the dogs, whose purpose was to cause the birds to rise, thus presenting the shooter with a target. This was very strenuous. It was not unusual, according to Maxwell, for the shooter who walked up behind a pointer to get up at 2am. Furthermore, it was a considerable gamble whether or not the bird could be shot. This method was gradually replaced by a new technique known as 'driving the game'. This consisted in the game being driven up to a line of butts, the purpose of which is to conceal the shooters while the beaters drive the coveys over the waiting guns, making them, as Maxwell says, 'unmissable targets'. Consequently shooting over the dogs was derided as a dead bore. With the driving method all the hard work is done by the beaters and flankers.

Driving was most successful where the moors were fairly level; in the mountainous regions it was more difficult. The moors of Derbyshire and Yorkshire were particularly suitable. George Sykes, Mr Henry Saville's keeper, of Rushworth Lodge, was the earliest master of the craft, although it is claimed that driving originated on moors west of the Flouch Inn near Penistone in 1804.[4]

But the final thing which resulted in driving becoming universal was the agricultural depression of the 1880s. According to Douglas Sutherland in *The Landowners*, 'The price of English wheat dropped by half. Wheat was pouring in from the American prairie farms, and from Canada and Australia. With improved refrigeration techniques cheap beef from the Argentine became a practical proposition. Danish eggs and bacon were pervading the English market for the first time.' The result by 1896 was that rents on average were 41 per cent below what they had been in 1873. Instead of using their wealth to combat the crisis by improving agricultural techniques most of the aristocracy continued their existing lifestyle.

Yet the old days, when the great landowners were able to maintain huge stocks of game for their pleasure and the amusement of guests, were passing away. Now they saw an opportunity for recouping their fortunes by catering for the hunting and shooting aspirations of the up-and-coming British industrialists and of the American millionaires. Not only had they the money and plenty of it, but more importantly they had royal patronage. As Brian Vesey-FitzGerald writes in *Vanishing Wild Life*, 'Not a few gentleman farmers now realised it was more profitable and infinitely less laborious to live off their syndicates than off their farms, but to do so they had of course to provide their clients with a more plentiful supply of game.'

Up to the mid-1880s, write Malcolm and Maxwell, the rents of the best moors were insignificant, but by 1910 they had increased ten-fold. They claim that one and a half million grouse were now being killed in a season. Mr A.S. Leslie, Secretary of the Grouse Disease Enquiry Committee, writing in 1910 estimated that the average yield from the grouse moors in Scotland, England and Wales was 1,220,000 brace and the rents were £1,250,000.

Maxwell states that 'driving' resulted in an increase of up to 800 per cent in the bags. Before that, according to Vesey FitzGerald in *Vanishing Wild Life*, forty-four grouse in a day's sport was regarded as the achievement of a lifetime, but in 1888 Lord Walsingham shot 1,070 grouse in one day on Blubberhouses Moor near Harrogate in Yorkshire. He had twenty drivers, divided into two parties of ten each. The noble Lord had plenty of aristocratic competition: the Marquis of Ripon claimed he had shot 556,800 head of game, while Earl D. Grey claimed 370,728. The era of record bags had now arrived. As Vesey-FitzGerald notes, the rich men who came from the south wanted to do much more than shoot grouse, they wanted to shoot lots and lots of grouse, grouse in their hundreds. The more grouse on the moor the higher the rent obtained. Even the moors themselves became involved in this competitiveness. Broomhead Moors, 4,000 acres in the Peak District, produced 5,000 grouse on August 30th 1893, more than one grouse per acre; other moors could only manage one grouse in every four or five acres. Wemmergill, a moor of 14,000 acres near Barnard Castle, produced 17,073 grouse in 1872.

This craze for record bags was taken to absurd lengths. Ivor Thomson, writing in *Shooting Times*, 28 July 1973, reported a conversation he had with Kit Pullen, who 'had been driving when Lord Walsingham created his record of 1,070 grouse to his own gun in one butt. The birds were driven backwards and forwards, and Pullen alleged towards the end of the day, men killed more tired game with their flagsticks than were shot.' There are many who regard this urge to achieve record kills as nauseating and degenerate, far removed from the days when hunting was necessary for the maintenance of life. Now all danger from the quarry had been eliminated and, owing to the 'mobbing of the game', the greatest danger was from fellow shooters! The Duke of Roxburghe was shot in the face by the 7th Lord Chesterfield, which resulted in the blood running down his Grace's shirt.[5] Possibly the most amusing incident was when the Prince of Wales accidentally shot Lord Clermont. *The Times* recording the incident wrote: 'twenty three and a half grains of number 4 shot were extracted from his Lordship's bum'.[6]

The ramblers were not the only ones adversely affected by this excessive game rearing. In fact the first to suffer were the farmers, already feeling the pinch from the agricultural depression. Land-owners found tenants, writes Vesey-FitzGerald, 'who could afford much more to shoot grouse than farmers could pay to graze sheep. Game-keepers came to the moors and shepherds could no longer do as they desired. . . . Shepherds like to delay the burning of the heather to the last legal date.' This, according to Vesey-FitzGerald, led to the grouse moor disasters of 1872 and 1873.

Both Royce and Ward state that the number of sheep in the Peak District had fallen: 'The old native will point to 50,000 sheep on the moorlands betwen Longdendale and Baslow sixty years ago, but who could find 5,000 there today?' writes Royce.[7] Hutchinson in his *Tour through the Peak in 1809* wrote of finding '. . . immense flocks of sheep.' Also he never encountered a keeper. So determined were the grouse moor owners to eliminate sheep from the grouse moors that, Malcolm and Maxwell report, one owner sought an injunction against a farmer for allowing sheep to stray on his grouse moor, but Justice Darling came down on the side of the sheep, because they provided more food. This did not stop the closing down of farms, nor did it restrain grouse moor owners claiming, as did the Reverend Macpherson, that by good management of the moors the food producing power could be increased.

Ward reprinted the wording on a notice board erected by the owner of a Derbyshire grouse moor which read:

> NOTICE. The public is warned that game is preserved on this land. You are therefore requested not to wander from the path and so help to protect that, which provides sport for some, trade for others and, in some measure, food for all.[8]

As Edwin Royce wrote, 'Six million people in this country who can only afford 6 shillings per week on food certainly do not include this bird in their diet.'[9]

Detrimental as extensive game rearing has been to some humans, for some wild animals it has been fatal. Some species, such as the white-tailed eagle have been wiped out. Vesey-FitzGerald states that they had a range far exceeding the golden eagle, even nesting in the Isle of Wight, but were much more plentiful in the north than the golden eagle. A predator of game it was also considered by shepherds to be a menace to sheep. They along with gamekeepers have exterminated it. Other species after suffering this fate have only been reintroduced after the most strenuous efforts and precautions made to preserve them. 'Many and various — large and small — are the animals waging war on our gallant little grouse', writes Maxwell. Vesey-FitzGerald, Vice-President of the Gamekeepers' Association and one-time editor of *The Field*, wrote: 'Gamekeepers of old regarded everything that was not game as vermin . . . 33 species of predatory birds, all of them which are shot . . . by gamekeepers.' Tom Speedy, author of *Sport in the Highlands and Lowlands of Scotland* (1886) put the golden eagle, which half a century ago existed in great numbers, at the head of the list of birds of prey; included are birds such as the hobby and the honey buzzard, which Vesey-FitzGerald states is harmless to game.

But the biggest task was to keep humans off the grouse moors. Macpherson writes: 'A grouse moor can hardly be kept too quiet in the breeding season, that is why the proprietors object so strongly to the intrusion of tourists being forced upon them by radical legislation.' (No doubt he was referring to Bryce's bill of 1884). Picozzi in 1967 made a three years' study

> . . . to investigate complaints from moor owners in the Peak District National Park that recent agreements, which allow people to walk over moorland areas away from public rights-of-way, had resulted in a decline in the numbers of Red Grouse shot each year. Broods of Red Grouse were counted on study areas on three moors where access was limited to rights-of-way. Past bags of the grouse shot on fifteen moors were also examined. Grouse breed no worse on study areas than on moors where people had unrestricted access, and grouse bags showed no evidence of a decline associated with public access agreements.[10]

Grouse soon become accustomed to crowds of people. The invasion of tourists in winter and summer near the ski lifts have little affected them. In the Cairngorms Cairnwell Watson has compared grouse stocks and their breeding on disturbed areas, alongside the lifts, with distant areas to which few people go, and has found no difference between stocks in disturbed and undisturbed habitats in any year.[11]

If in England it was the grouse which gave rise to the social conflicts, in Scotland it was mainly the deer, though there are plenty of grouse. Few animals have had longer association with humans than the deer. Whereas in earlier times the deer was hunted for food, in recent centuries it has been 'the thrill of the kill' which has been the attraction. With the exception of Exmoor, truly wild deer are scarce in England and Wales, but in Scotland their numbers today are greater than for many years.

Following the defeat of the Jacobite army at Culloden in 1746, the crofters of the Highland Glens were evicted to make way firstly for the southern sheep graziers, followed by deer forests, which gave even better returns. Many thousand crofters were evicted to give place to shepherds. Most were compelled to emigrate. Eviction reached a maximum during the first half of the nineteenth century. Glens once populous became almost uninhabited owing to the decrease in the price of wool and mutton resulting from imports from Australia. From the middle of the nineteenth century, many sheep pastures were being converted to deer forests. The few shepherds were replaced by an even smaller number of stalkers and the result was hunger and misery. In addition to forced emigration, many were driven into the rising industrial towns of central Scotland.

From the late seventeenth century to the eighteenth there was great hunger in the farmlands: famine killed off half the population in some Deeside parishes.[12] It was the industrial revolution which enormously extended the deer forests, making them playgrounds of the wealthy. Queen Victoria and her consort Prince Albert, with their purchase of Balmoral in 1848, set the pattern, resulting in the building of many shooting lodges for the wealthy industrialists, both English and foreign. According to Grimble, by 1890 they numbered just over 150, covering two and a half million acres of land, although in their heyday there were four million acres. They still cover about two and three quarter million acres, with the red deer ranging over seven million acres, or 37 per cent of Scotland's land.[13]

References to Chapter 3

1 Coppock, J.T., 'The Recreational Use of Land and Water in Rural Britian', *Journal of Economic and Social Geography*, 3 (1966), p88
2 *Scottish Field*, 1932

3 Trench, C.C., *The Poacher and the Squire*, (1967), p125
4 *Clarion Handbook*, 1939-40
5 Malcolm and Maxwell, *Grouse and Grouse Moors*, (1910), p140

6 Trench, C.C., *op cit*, p126

7 *Ramblers' Federation Handbook*, 1931

8 *Clarion Handbook*, 1936-7

9 *Ramblers' Association Gazette*, June 1937

10 Picozzi, N. 'Breeding Performance and Shooting Bags of Red Grouse in Relation to Public Access in the Peak District National Park, England' *Biological Conservation* III, 1 October 1970, pp211-5

11 Nethersole-Thompson, D, and Watson, A., *The Cairngorms: Their Natural History and Scenery*, (1974), p114

12 Ibid, p21

13 *Red Deer Commission Report*, 1972

4   Between the Two Wars

The twenty years which divided the two World Wars are the most important for the struggle of the rambling movement for access — not that it registered any success in securing legal access. Yet without this struggle the important Act of 1949 might never have reached the Statute Book.

Ramblers returning from the trenches, men and women leaving the munition factories, encouraged by the promises of a 'Brave New World' had every reason to believe that the post-war Parliament would quickly introduce a government bill conceding their justifiable demand, especially as the three main parties had already given their blessing to Trevelyan's and Bryce's 1908 Bills. They also treasured the hope that the grouse moor owners and syndicates would honour all the fine promises made on their behalf by Lloyd George, who had promised 'a land fit for heroes' to live in.

Instead of an end to the harassment on the grouse moors which had marred the pre-war scene, the ramblers received an even more hostile reception. The guns had been silenced for barely a year over the battlefields of Flanders, before they started booming over the grouse moors of the Peak. The gamekeepers launched the most violent attacks on the 'trespassing' ramblers on that most sacred of grouse moors, Kinder Scout — whose very name epitomizes the sixty years of access struggle.

The *Clarion Handbook* for 1921-2 carries a letter from a correspondent:

> I have observed . . . gamekeepers in Sunday clothes are watching at Edale Station the arrival of Sheffield and Manchester Sunday morning trains, and to see if ramblers attempt to climb any part of Kinder Scout, and leave the roundabout footpaths, which do not reveal half the glory of that famous plateau and rock edge . . . there are men fixed at various points on the top to signal and intercept and turn men back — as though they were thieves.[1]

One of the five owners was a Mr Watt, warehouse merchant of Manchester. In the 1890s he was Vice-Chairman of the Hayfield and Kinder Scout Ancient Footpaths Association, which succeeded in forcing the re-opening of the Kinder Scout footpath. Later he purchased a part of the Scout and used it as a grouse moor. The only access he allowed was by permit, which was exceedingly difficult to obtain. Following the death in January 1922 of H.F. Martin in a south-west gale on Kinder Scout and the death of Edward Newton during February of the same year he refused to allow any access at all to the summit.

On 30 April 1933 Watt inserted in the Manchester evening paper an

14   *Kinder Downfall in the Peak District could only be visited by a select few with permit in 1920, and even this was withdrawn in 1922.*

15   *A permit to visit Kinder Downfall in 1920.*

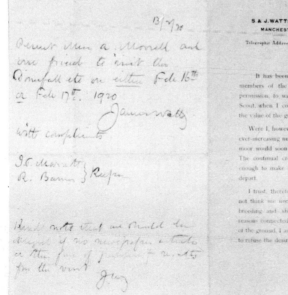

advertisement offering a £5 reward to anyone who could identify any of the persons whose photographs were included in the advertisement. The advertisement caused such an outcry — editorially in a Manchester newspaper and to the solicitors who received hundreds of protesting letters — that no similar advertisement ever appeared again. This in no way deterred Watt. G.H.B. Ward reports that in 1923-4 there were about six gamekeepers employed on the top during the summer and autumn weekends to chase off any ramblers venturing on to Kinder Scout.

16   *The 1933 Manchester newspaper advertisement which caused an outcry.*

It was Ward who in these early years was the *bête noir* of all Peak landowners and gamekeepers. He referred to them as the 'Mussolini of the hills' after he had been confronted by a gamekeeper, brandishing a stick, who had no hesitation in declaring that 'this is the way to deal with ***** Socialists.'[2] Watt reinforced this restrictive attitude by having a writ served on Ward, restraining him from going on Kinder Scout; since Ward was a civil servant he 'had to apologise and promise not to trespass again on that Holy Land'. Officially he never went on that moor again for ten years — until the owner died in the early 'thirties.[3]

Ward and the Clarion Ramblers were not the only ones to attempt to breach the battlements of Kinder. Very quickly the pre-war association with the Manchester ramblers was resumed. The first 'intermeet' with Mac's Ramblers of Manchester was on Sunday 16 May 1920, when they went up Kinder via Jacob's Ladder. Barely another four months were to elapse before they were again challenging Lord Howard's stoppage of the ancient Doctor's Gate track. Later, rambling clubs from other towns joined in. These 'joint raids', as G.H.B. Ward had called them, were the precursors of a relationship which was destined to have a profound effect on the whole future of rambling, and the struggle for access.

The *Ramblers' Federation Handbook* (1928) reported two demonstration walks over a disputed path at Benfield near Hyde, attended by 2,500 people; during these walks a formidable obstruction was removed. At about the same time, Sheffield ramblers were turned back from walking along Baslow, Curbar and Froggatt Edges — one of the most beautiful three miles in Derbyshire. Every edge in the Peak was a trespass area, being closely guarded by the gamekeepers. To defy them was the only way to enjoy the panoramic views.

In the years following the end of World War I, many thousands more sought to enjoy the invigorating rejuvenation which the early ramblers experienced, especially as conditions in the industrial towns grew harsher. This was the period of mass unemployment and wage cuts, which led to the only general strike ever to have occurred in Britain. As the employed and unemployed flooded into Derbyshire, the attacks by the gamekeepers became more numerous. Edwin Royce writing in the *Handbook* of the Manchester Federation, reported how three walkers crossing Bleaklow were confronted by an infuriated gamekeeper brandishing a revolver, and this, apparently, was not the first time. Stephen Morton recalls how on the struggle to reopen Doctor's Gate they were met by keepers with clubs and fierce dogs; a few were brandishing shot guns. There were hundreds of incidents, most of them unreported. Not that the ramblers went out in order to have a fight with the keepers. What they wanted was a respite from the 'pull and push' of factory and city life.

Nonetheless, deliberate trespassing did occur on an increasing scale in spite of threats of injunctions and the vicious attacks of the keepers. Trespassing became an art, part of which was to dodge the keepers, the other was to do no damage:

> The ethic of nice trespassing is based, like all ethics, on the true consideration for the proper feelings of others. No 'Compleat trespasser', for instance, would invade the privacy of a fellow man. One does not take short cuts across the lawn of a suburban villa. One does not damage fences or trample crops.

There were no greater opponents of vandalism than the organised ramblers.

No less a figure than C.P. Trevelyan, in a speech to London ramblers reported in the *Yorkshire Post*, 14 December 1925, urged ramblers, who he declared were good citizens, to be ready to break the so-called trespass law, which in fact did not exist. For as Justice MacKinnon said during the hearing of a civil action at the Chester Assizes: ' "Trespassers will be prosecuted" was no longer enforceable since the Act passed during the reign of George II had been repealed. "I trespass about once a week" said his lordship amid laughter.' (*Chester Courant,* 8 November 1933). It is for this reason that Ward and Royce dubbed 'Trespassers will be Prosecuted' notice boards as 'wooden lies'. Furthermore, one thing that ramblers could not understand was that they were guilty of trespass or damage for walking across wild moorland, while fox-hunters could pursue their prey across the cultivated countryside with little or no opposition.

Northern ramblers were a determined lot! They had a deeply held conviction that right and natural justice based on ancient usage were on their side. Equally determined were many gamekeepers, abusive, sometimes armed with guns, always with thick sticks, which they were not loath to use. If this view of gamekeepers is considered unfair, read what Brian Vesey-FitzGerald, Vice-President of the Game Keepers' Association, had to say about them in his two books, *Vanishing Wild Life of Britain* and *British Game.* He wrote that the gamekeeper 'Who flourished in the 80s and 90s and into the opening years of this century, was from all accounts a rather terrible person, quite uneducated, . . . frequently brutal!' Sir Peter Jeffrey Mackie, whom Vesey-Fitzgerald credited in 1929 with knowing more about

17   Bleaklow Head. This 37 square miles of rough moorland was untraversed by a single public right of way until the establishment of the Pennine Way. In the 1920s ramblers were chased off by a gamekeeper armed with a revolver.

keepers than anybody else, considered the percentage of trustworthy gamekeepers as not very high. Very much akin it would seem to Black George in Fielding's *Tom Jones*.

One may consider it unfair to blame those keepers who fell into this category. The real culprits were those who employed them, for woe betide any keeper who was lax in carrying out his employer's instructions. According to the Duke of Devonshire's head keeper, there were around sixty keepers in the Peak District. They received a wage which was not much greater than that paid to the labourers working for the Derwent Valley Water Board, but in addition each had a rent-free cottage, plus a suit of clothes and food for his dogs.

It was not only on the grouse moors that the ramblers were being given a more hostile reception. As against the friendly reception given to the 1908 Access to Mountains bills, Parliament simply refused to discuss the six bills which were introduced between 1920 and 1931.

Outside Parliament, support was growing from the increasing number of open-air enthusiasts and the press, especially the *Manchester Guardian*. On 21 April 1925 this newspaper included a piece which has probably been quoted more times than any other by supporters of access:

> There is something wantonly perverse and profane in a society in which the rights of property can be used to defeat the emotions in which mankind has found its chief inspiration and comfort. If ever any truth lurked in the phrase 'the rights of man' those rights should surely include the right to climb the mountains, and the right to dream beside the sea.

But *The Times* was strongly opposed. What is surprising for a paper which has always claimed to be so well informed was its comment of 14 May 1924:

> The grievance which it purports to remove has little real existence. It is a bogey in the imagination of certain dwellers in the town to whom the secrets of the countryside are a sealed book, simply because they do not care to turn its pages. . . .Those who love the country itself, who delight in long walks, know well enough by experience that, for example, in the wilder parts of Scotland and Wales and the Lake District and the Dales, they are free enough to wander where they like, provided they show a due consideration for the convenience and the rights of other peoples.[8]

Even if the Sheffield and Manchester ramblers could walk freely in the Lake District how did this help those thousands who visited Derbyshire on a week-end, many of whom were on low wages and unemployed, and could not afford the fares to get further afield?

Royce, writing in the 1931 *Ramblers' Federation Handbook*, asserted that 10,000 people were seeking fresh air in Derbyshire on any week-end. Special ramblers' trains and other forms of public transport were negotiated by the Federation to convey walkers to the nearest suburban termini. According to a BBC broadcast in this period entitled 'Northern Cockpit', a Sheffield railway station issued 30,000 tickets in the month of August for people travelling to Derbyshire stations. In one week Sheffield buses conveyed 4,351 people to Derwent and Ashopton. Others without the fare walked all the way.

At the height of what has been dubbed the 'rambling craze' in the early 1930s, estimates of the number of open-air enthusiasts varied upwards to half a million. By this time there existed in Britain a national body of ramblers known as the National Council of Ramblers' Federations, formed in 1930. It had emerged following a preliminary meeting held at Hope, in Derbyshire, to discuss the setting up of such a body.[9] Local federations of affiliated clubs existed in Liverpool, Manchester, Sheffield, London, North-East Lancashire, Nottingham and Derbyshire, Staffordshire, Lincolnshire, Bristol, Cumberland, Scotland, Bolton and Huddersfield. The first local federation to be formed was in and around London in 1905. Its primary, and it would seem only, purpose was to negotiate cheap circular rail and bus transport, and also provide lists of catering establishments. Not so the northern federations. Stephen Morton of the Sheffield Federation has said that this body gave them greater power in the fight for access.

One of the earliest northern federations was formed in Liverpool in 1922. It was committed by a clause in its constitution 'to urge the public right of access to moors and mountains.' Increasing concern was shown by this federation at the growing loss of footpaths in the Wirral owing to building operations and obstructions placed by land owners and farmers. To counter these actions the federations organised a series of 'right-of-way rambles', many of which were attended by over a hundred ramblers. During one of these a gate obstructing a path was lifted from its hinges, which led to a writ being served by Lever Brothers, owners of the land, on one of the ramblers. After four young people had been fined for trespass the federation wrote to the Chief Constable contrasting the aid given by the police to owners of land with their refusal to take any action against illegal obstruction of rights of way, but this had no effect.

By 1933 thirty-six clubs were affiliated to the Liverpool Federation. They included the   As You Like It Club, Scouts, Holiday Fellowship, Independent Labour Party Guild of Youth, and the Workers Educational Association. The Merseyside Region of the Youth Hostels Association started the youth hostelling movement in Britain in 1929. In that year, following a visit by seven Liverpool ramblers to the youth shelters in Germany, the Liverpool Federation set up a committee of three to explore the idea. This was followed by the federation convening a meeting on December 12 which decided to proceed with the formation of a local Youth Hostels Association. The first hostel was opened at Christmas 1930 at Pennant Hall in the Conway Valley, but it had only a brief existence.

It was not until 1930 that a Ramblers' Federation was formed in Birmingham. Affiliated to it were between thirty and forty clubs which included the 36-year-old Midland Institute of Ramblers, the Coventry Holiday Fellowship and the Walsall Rambling Club.

The Manchester and Sheffield Ramblers' Federations   It was the

Manchester and Sheffield federations that were the major inspirers and organisers of access agitation. The Manchester and District Federation was formed in 1922 by a fusion of the Rambling Council dating from 1919 — the first organisation of its kind in Manchester — with another organisation known as the Manchester and District Federation of Ramblers, started in 1921. While it undertook all the functions of arranging cheap fares, special trains and a list of catering facilities, embodied in its constitution were two objectives: to urge the right of access to mountains and moors and to spread information regarding ancient public highways.

So highly rated in the Manchester Federation's priorities was the fight for 'Access to our grand moorlands and mountains', that they formed a special committee 'whose duty it was to mould public opinion to our way of thinking — no easy task.'[10] The Committee began this task by circularising forty-nine candidates standing in the 1922 General Election, enquiring: 'in the event of your election will you be willing to co-operate in the introduction of a Bill to give free public access to moors and mountains?'

Manchester influence reached far wider than the city itself. Clubs from Sheffield, Leeds, Derby, Nottingham, Stoke-on-Trent, Blackpool, Barnsley, and Lancaster were affiliated to the Manchester Federation; all areas which are covered by the term Northern. It started out with thirty-seven affiliated clubs; by the height of the rambling boom in 1932, that number had trebled.

It is interesting to try and estimate the strata of the population on which the clubs were based. So far as this is possible it appears that Leonard's Co-operative Holidays Association, the Holiday Fellowship and the Naturalist Societies predominated. This is not surprising when it is remembered how much interest Manchester working men have had from the earliest days of the industrial revolution in the flora and fauna of the countryside. Colne, birthplace of the CHA, is not far from Manchester. What is more surprising is the number of rambling clubs based on religious institutions. Equally interesting, if less surprising, are the numbers of direct affiliations from the sections of the Labour movement, for example Gorton Independent Labour Party, Barnsley Trades Council and Co-operative Movement. The Manchester Federation also had affiliations from the Boy Scouts and the Rambling Club for the Blind, Manchester.

The year 1923 saw the beginning of the *Ramblers' Federation Handbook,* a publication which during its sixteen years' existence reflected the justice of the claim for access, recording all the stages in the development of the rambling movement, directing attention to specific acts of illegal closure of footpaths, and giving details of ramblers' transport and catering facilities. Its editor was Edwin Royce, whose determined fight for access in the Peak and Scotland was based on a deep understanding of the vested interests which blocked the realization of man's basic desire to walk upon the land in which he or she is born.

The Sheffield Federation was formed in 1926 of eighteen affiliated clubs, and while never as big as the Manchester Federation, was strongly for access. It was Ward's indefatigable research which revealed the injustice of the enclosures, not all of which had had Parliamentary sanction; this research provided ammunition for the staunch ramblers who formed the hard core of the Sheffield rambling fraternity. They passionately believed that all people had the right to walk on the grouse moors, so pithily summed up in Ward's questioning phrase 'Who wants a footpath when you can manage without one?' They never shirked a struggle to re-open or preserve a right of way that Ward's investigation had revealed to have been arbitrarily taken away.

18 *The access demonstration in the Winnats Pass, Castleton, Derbyshire, organised by the Manchester and Sheffield Ramblers' Federations.*

With these two bases, Manchester and Sheffield, providing both the intellectual basis of the movement and the bulk of the man and woman power, it is not surprising that the access struggle reached a high level of intensity between the mid-twenties and mid-thirties. The first public demonstration of ramblers in support of Trevelyan's Access Bill took place in the Winnats Pass, Castleton, Derbyshire, on 12 June 1926. It was considered by the Manchester Federation to have been highly successful.

Every year until 1939 there were similar demonstrations which were jointly organised with the Sheffield Federation. They became so successful, with an estimated 8,000 at the 1929 demonstration, that the *Daily Express* moved in, loaning amplifying equipment and providing community song sheets. To one of these demonstrations both Ramsay Macdonald and Lloyd George sent letters of support, but significantly did nothing to aid Trevelyan's efforts in Parliament. The Liverpool Federation held demonstrations for many years from 1927, for instance on Saturday 23 June 1928 2,000

19   *The Cobbler, Arrochar, near Loch Long where in the 1930s the caves in these mountains were the 'howffs' of the Glaswegian climbers.*

ramblers attended a demonstration at Thurstaston Hill, the Wirral.

Scotland   In no part of Britain was the urge to leave the towns greater than that experienced by those living in the industrial regions of Scotland. The slums of Glasgow were notorious for their squalor. And the conditions of work — when it could be had — were no less arduous than those experienced in industrial England. Equally important, within easy reach

59

was a countryside of unrivalled beauty which attracted thousands of urban dwellers. The journalist mountaineer Tom Weir, writing in the *Scots Magazine* about the early 1930s, has likened the consequent exodus to a 'great outdoor revolution'. 'On Sunday mornings', he says, 'youngsters like myself would catch the bus to Blanefield for a day on the Campsie Fells.'

For the more venturesome such a day was a soft option. After a long day's work finishing around 9pm they preferred to set out at night when, as John Nimlin wrote in the *Scottish Mountaineering Club Journal*, May 1963, 'most of the long distance trains and buses had retired'. They arrived at all hours of the night and early morning at their destinations, which were the more distant parts of Ben Lomond or the Cobbler, situated among the rocky escarpments of the Arrochar Mountains. They used various means of cheap transport. Sometimes it was 'the covered wagon type' of lorry, 'murderously cold in the winter, but always overloaded, and not entirely legal in use.' This later gave way to the club bus. The real down-and-outs claimed to have originated the 'thumbed lift'. When this failed they had no alternative but to do the 'fifteen miles long slog to Loch Achray' weighed down with a heavy pack. They scorned even the spartan comforts of the newly established youth hostels, preferring as 'howffs' the lofts in lowly cottages. And infinitely more attractive were the caves in the hills which would then become the stage for a wild Scots *ceilidh*.

> Bruce's cave in Glen Lion, Arrochar, was the most popular 'howff' in the west. At one time it recorded more bednights than the youth hostel in the Glen below. Countless songs were roared around its confines as the smoke billowed through the natural chimney in the cave roof. No Viking celebration was wilder than a cave man's gathering, with up to fifty climbers in the company, and all the surrounding caves and overhangs booked to capacity.

Apart from the fire they kept warm by the close proximity of their fellow revellers, sometimes aided by the news-sheets of the *Glasgow Herald*.

These were the tough characters who formed the Creag Dhu, the Cragiallon Boys and the Ptarmigan. Drawn from the opposite ends of the social scale from the longer established professional mountaineering clubs, they were nonetheless very exclusive. The membership of the Ptarmigan Club was limited to twenty. It was so named, writes Nimlin, 'not for the spur by that name on Ben Lomond, but for the tough little bird of the high tops whose most southerly outpost is the summit of the Ben itself.' Nimlin's first acquaintance with the leader of the Creag Dhu, Andy Sellars, was when he emerged from 'the top, to say goodbye forever to that particular rent' which was named Coffin Gulley.

Not all Glaswegians found relief from the smoke and grime of the Clyde basin in the mystique of the modern weekend cave-dwelling communities. Many more were happy enough to enjoy a walk where 'every ramble was a radiant venture in a newly created world.'

At this period, whereas the newly formed climbing clubs were few, about seventy rambling clubs were affiliated to the Scottish Federation, two-thirds of the number affiliated to the Manchester and District Federation.

There were three district councils: Glasgow, Aberdeen, Edinburgh-and-Fife. The Federation was affiliated to the National Council. There were the usual clubs linked with the churches, literary societies and the Labour movement but the most unusual were the Imperialist Club, the Deutschsprechende Wanderer and the Esperanto Club.[11]

Scottish clubs, too, had their differences with the keepers and police. In the Renfrewshire hills which Tom Weir writes were 'possessively keepered', he and a companion were brutally assaulted by an ugly pair: 'we parted, blood streaming from my friend's swollen nose and my shirt torn where it had been seized.' Nor were these isolated incidents; police raids were common 'on those who stole into derelict cottages and outhouses, when the delights of Loch Lomond and Loch Katrine were being discovered' by hikers and cyclists. Similar incidents are reported in the *Scottish Ramblers' Handbook,* published in the 1930s, which resulted in the Scottish Federation setting out as one of its objects the demand for 'access to mountains and moors'. A mass meeting was held in St Andrews Hall and a rally on Scotstown Moor. Nevertheless, in this century the movement for access in Scotland has never reached the intensity of that in the Peak. The major reason being that whereas in the Peak the grouse moors were on the doorstep of the northern industrial towns, the best deer forests and grouse moors were not so accessible to the central belt of Scotland's industrial towns.

References to Chapter 4

1 *Clarion Handbook*, 1921-2
2 Ibid, 1928-9
3 Ibid, 1958-9
4 Ibid, 1954-5
5 Ibid, 1927-8
6 Ibid, 1924-5
7 *Ramblers' Federation Handbook* 1929
8 Ibid, 1927
9 *Clarion Handbook*, 1931-2
10 *25 Milestones*, Ramblers' Association, Manchester and District Federation (1948)
11 *Scottish Ramblers' Federation Handbook*, 1930, 1931, 1932, 1935

5   The Mass Trespasses

Kinder Scout   The great event which shook the rambling world in the early 1930s was the Kinder Scout mass trespass. The official ramblers' movement had tried everything they knew, yet they were further away from their goal of gaining access than was James Bryce forty years back. He had won an affirmative vote for the right of access from a Parliament less representative of the ordinary people than were the post-war ones. What to do next? — that was the puzzling question in every rambler's mind.

It was a young unemployed motor mechanic from Manchester, Bernard Rothman, who along with a group of his friends, organised in the British Workers Sports Federation, supplied the answer. On a fine morning, Sunday 24 April 1932, a party of ramblers, estimated by Rothman between '600 to 800 — probably round about that mark',[1] (the police put the number 'at about 200', the *Daily Express* 500[2]) set off from Hayfield, a village nestling in the Peak, to storm openly the fortress of Britain's most sacred grouse moor — the 2,000 feet high plateau of Kinder Scout. After a brief skirmish with stick-wielding gamekeepers, they achieved their objective. History had been made. They had, in full view of the police, walked on ground which up to 100 years before had been free land, proof of which has already been established from the earlier quotations from G.H.B. Ward, Dr E.A. Baker and the publication from the Hayfield and Kinder Scout Ancient Footpaths Association.

Little did Rothman and his friends realise what they had started. The rambling world was ablaze with excitement and controversy. There were those who were outraged with a Parliament which had in Ramsay Macdonald a Prime Minister who declared himself to be more committed to legal access than any of his predecessors, yet refused to give facilities for the discussion of Ellen Wilkinson's 1931 Bill. They saw in the Mass Trespass a new round of direct-action skirmishes which would compel the small but influential landowning and grouse shooting interests to give way. There were others, such as Harold Wild of the Manchester and District Ramblers' Federation and Stephen Morton, secretary of the Sheffield Federation, who declared it had set the campaign 'back 20 years, at a time when we were beginning to break the power of the owners and getting them to meet us across the conference table.' Whichever view was held, there is no doubt all organised ramblers admired, as Tom Stephenson said, the courage of Rothman and his friends. They were particularly outraged by the prison sentences which five of the mass trespassers received later at the Derby Assizes.

The idea of a Mass Trespass arose out of a ramble which started from a camp for young people at Rowarth, south of Glossop, organised by the Lancashire District of the Workers Sports Federation, a body started on the initiative of the Young Communist League in Manchester. A number of these camps had taken place earlier, and this particular ramble was going from Rowarth over Bleaklow. They were stopped by gamekeepers, and this caused much annoyance. During the ensuing discussion there emerged the idea that 'They might have stopped a few of us but they'll not stop the lot of us'.[1] Bernard Rothman is unable to say which of the incensed ramblers uttered the historic words 'Mass Trespass'. He is certain these two words were the collective response, arising out of the injustice to which they had been subjected.

Rothman and his friends felt so deeply aggrieved at the denial of access by a handful of grouse shooters, and by the failure of the official campaign by the National Council of the Ramblers' Association to make any progress, that nothing short of an open public demonstration upon Kinder Scout would do. Whereupon they planned the biggest public campaign possible.

On 18 April 1932, Rothman visited the offices of the *Manchester Evening News*. Next day the plans were headlined: 'Mass Trespass over Kinder Scout', embellished with emotive phrases like 'Assaults' and 'Shock Troops'. The rest of the press immediately took it up. At the end of the week leaflets were distributed which put the ramblers' case succinctly: 'It is a crime for workers to put their feet where Lord Big Bug, and Lady Little Flea do their annual shooting.'

But the Manchester Ramblers' Federation condemned the trespass, urging their members not to take part. This did not stop a few officials and many of their club members joining the Trespass, for it was not the first time some of them had walked over prohibited ground, or faced abusive gamekeepers. Meanwhile the grouse moor owners were busy making their own preparations. A number of regular gamekeepers, including the Duke of Devonshire's head keeper, were assisted by a few temporary keepers. In total, according to Rothman, there were around eighteen, although the *Daily Express* put the number at sixty,[2] as did the *Daily Herald*. They were all supplied with the usual gamekeepers' heavy sticks. Most important of all were the police. Sergeant Brailsford was one of the policemen there, and when interviewed after his retirement he said there were about thirty police, as well as a number of plain clothes officials. He said the presence of Superintendent Garrow, Deputy Chief Constable of Derbyshire, indicated how seriously the police regarded the Trespass. The *Sheffield Independent* of Monday 25 April claimed that Hayfield was alive with police, a number of whom were hidden in the local cinema.

Before even the Mass Trespass started, efforts were made by the police to prevent Rothman getting there. They were waiting at the Manchester and Hayfield railway stations with an injunction restraining him from attending the Hayfield meeting, which had been advertised to precede the actual Trespass. Unfortunately for the police, he and one other, knowing nothing of this, went to Hayfield on their bicycles, and walked along the route which they had planned the Trespass should take; when he arrived at Hayfield to hold the advertised meeting a dense crowd had already assembled.

The police under the command of the Deputy Chief Constable ringed the recreation ground, and they had already been in action stopping the playing of leap-frog. They had with them the Parish Clerk to read the regulations which had been newly posted, prohibiting the holding of meetings. This was quite unnecessary, for Rothman and his friends quickly realised that if they attempted to hold the meeting on the recreation ground it would be the start and finish of the Trespass. Accordingly word was passed round to leave the recreation ground and to move along William Clough up towards Kinder along a path which had been the object of a twenty year struggle to force its re-opening at the end of the last century.

This initiative took the police quite by surprise, and before they realised what was happening, the ramblers were disappearing along the track, followed by perspiring bobbies, unaccustomed to moorland tramping. The first stop was near the Kinder Reservoir, but officials belonging to the Stockport Corporation Waterworks dashed along and banned it. As the Mass Trespassers' quarrel was not with them, they carried on until they reached an old disused quarry, a natural amphitheatre. There Rothman addressed the ramblers, insisting the trespass was to be orderly, disciplined and non-

20   *Bernard Rothman addressing the ramblers in the quarry during the 1932 mass trespass on Kinder Scout.*

21 The mass trespassers marching to Kinder on 24 April 1932.

violent. To ensure it was so, as Rothman explained later in his trial at Derby, he instructed them how they were to proceed once they left the footpath. One long blast meant advance in open order, the object being to walk round the keepers. This is in fact what happened to the overwhelming majority of the 800 ramblers, as was verified by Police Inspector Clews, the chief witness at the trials. 'The fight' he said 'took place over a front of twenty yards', only a handful of ramblers being involved, while the others made for the top.

At the quarry meeting everybody was determined that the trespass must go ahead, despite the presence of the police and gamekeepers. 'Away we went', says Rothman,

> singing along William Clough, so strong, it was impossible for the police to stop us — there were too many of us. It was a really dense crowd of young people, all picturesque in rambling gear, khaki jackets, khaki shirts, abbreviated shorts, colourful shorts, colourful jerseys — away we went in a jubilant mood, determined to carry out the assault on Kinder, also determined that no authority whatever would stop us.

The outwitted police were intent on stopping the trespass, hoping to isolate Rothman and pick up any stragglers. But it was not to be — the ramblers guarded him, and at every stile the main body did not move off until everybody was through. It wasn't planned, explains Rothman, it just happened.

At the Sandy Heys Moor — the pre-determined point — a long blast on the whistle heralded the beginning of the trespass. All the girls and youths left the path, crossed the stream and dashed up the steep side of Kinder. Some were met by gamekeepers holding out their sticks which they used to belabour the advancing ramblers, other ramblers stood back aghast at the violence used by the keepers. Those attacked used their rucksacks as shields seizing what sticks they could, breaking them, and then following the others onto the crest of the plateau. There they met contingents from Sheffield and Stockport who had carried out a trouble-free trespass across Kinder. 'There we exchanged congratulations, held a short victory meeting and held a little council of war', for Rothman sensed this wasn't by any means the end. For, in addition to the police they had seen at Hayfield, the Sheffield reinforcements told how they had observed numerous police en route.

They decided to return as they came in a solid body, 'full of determination, full of solidarity in maintaining our same tactics of waiting at every stile to

22   *The ramblers returning from the Kinder trespass.*

prevent arrest', which they did. About one mile before reaching Hayfield they met the police who were stretched right across the road. The gamekeepers, accompanied by the police, moved amongst the ranks of the ramblers and picked out five who they claimed were responsible for the melée — the sixth had been arrested early after the scuffle, and was later charged with causing grievous bodily harm to Beevers, one of the temporary keepers. They were taken to the Hayfield Lock-up, but because of the efforts of the ramblers to release them — hammering on the door and threatening to break the Police Station down — they were transferred to New Mills and kept there overnight.

Next day the six of them were charged at New Mills Police Court with unlawful assembly and breach of the peace. The six charged were John T. Anderson, Julius Clyne, Harry Mendel, Walter Gillet, Bernard Rothman and David Nussbaum. John Anderson was further charged with doing grievous bodily harm to temporary keeper Beevers. They were remanded to a special court on 11 May. After three adjournments at the Petty Divisional Court the accused were finally committed to the Assizes at Derby. By then all their witnesses had dropped out of the case, as they could not afford the fare and expenses and lost time.

The trial was held at Derby on 7 and 8 July when they were all charged with 'riotously assembling to disturb the public'. In addition John Anderson was also charged with maliciously inflicting grievous bodily harm on Edward Beevers, and there were seven other charges. The most extensive coverage of the trial appears in the *Derbyshire Advertiser*, 8 July 1932, where it is clear that the only evidence submitted of riotous assembly was the meeting in the recreation ground which in fact never took place. The police witness, Inspector Clews, under cross-examination agreed that 'the only people who had useful weapons were the keepers, and violence only occurred when the crowd met them.' In fact the only person on the landowners' side to suffer any injury was special keeper Beevers, and it was generally felt that it was he who provoked the struggle, using his stick. He tried what he called 'gentle persuasion' on John Anderson, who according to Detective Constable Christian was seen 'holding onto a keeper's stick as if he was trying to take it away from him.' The detective agreed that Anderson might have been trying to defend himself.

Police Constable Hudson, cross-examined by Rothman, who defended himself, agreed that Rothman did not incite the crowd to violence. On the contrary, the constable agreed, Rothman 'urged them to behave in a quiet and orderly manner.' Though other reports claim that Beevers was knocked unconscious and dragged by the crowd, following which he was taken to Stockport Infirmary, strangely enough he was not carried the two-mile journey to Hayfield, only 'assisted', according to Sergeant Brailsford, for part of the way. He returned home from hospital that same night.

The *Sheffield Independent* published a photograph of Beevers after the struggle being given a drink of water fetched by a rambler — hardly the act of a criminal. All the rest of the police evidence was calculated to play on the political prejudices of the jury, which was made up of two Brigadier-Generals, three Colonels, two Majors, three Captains, two Aldermen, all

23 Ramblers helping the gamekeeper Edward Beevers, injured during the Kinder trespass.

country gentlemen as quoted by C.E.M. Joad, *The Untutored Townsman's Invasion of the Country.* The evidence against Nussbaum was that he shouted that the *Daily Worker* (which he was selling) was the only paper supporting the Mass Trespass. Gillet, said Inspector Clews, had a copy of the *Communist Review* on him. In fact, so concerned was Judge Acton that the prosecution was turning the trial into a political one, that, in his summing up, he had to plead with the jury not to allow the 'extreme views of some of the prisoners (to) enter the case. Nor would they allow themselves in any way to be prejudiced because some of the men had names which sounded perhaps strange to members of the jury.' In view of the anti-semitic propaganda then current, he was clearly referring to the Jews: Rothman, Nussbaum and Clyne.

All with the exception of Mendel were found guilty, and received a total of seventeen months' imprisonment, Anderson receiving the longest sentence. Ironically, he went on the trespass to oppose it, but was so incensed with the brutality of certain of the keepers, that he got drawn into the melée.

There are some surprising things about the trial. Although the judge adopted a pose of fairness, his treatment of the defendants is questionable, and political prejudice loomed large in the case. There was no evidence of violence from the ramblers, as all the newspapers reporting the trespass agreed. What violence there was came from the keepers, who were provided with thick sticks for that purpose. In fact, the ramblers acted in a most exemplary way. The *Sheffield Telegraph* reporting on the trespass declared that hooliganism was entirely absent, gates were closed, orange peel and paper buried. Anderson got six months for assault, yet the police witness agreed he was trying to protect himself from being assaulted by the keeper, and the only injury Beever sustained was a twisted ankle, resulting from falling over. Because the defendants were five minutes later in getting back into the court after the first day's lunch break, due to their difficulty in finding a café, the judge, in Rothman's words, 'gave us a fearful lecture', and committed them to Leicester gaol for the night. It was in the semi-darkness of the cell that Bernard Rothman finished preparing his defence — and what a defence it was!

'We ramblers', he told the court, 'after a hard week's work and life in smoky towns and cities go out rambling for relaxation, a breath of fresh air, a little sunshine. We find, when we go out, that the finest rambling country is closed to us, because certain individuals wish to shoot for about ten days a year. For twenty-five years the Ramblers' Federation has carried on a campaign which has been futile. It was united action on the part of the ramblers that the well-known path, Doctor's Gate was opened'.

He went on to reveal the failure of the prosecution to prove its case:

We are not hooligans, we tried to avoid contact with the keepers by advancing in open formation. When the keepers raised their stick we took them from them... The mass trespass of April 24 was a peaceful demonstration of protest.

Abbey Brook   The second Mass Trespass took place five months after the first on Sunday 18 September 1932, across a much disputed right of way — the Duke of Norfolk's Road, which petered out into a path and bridleway terminating at Abbey Grange in the Derwent Valley. A full account of how the track was constructed and recognised as a right of way is given in the *Clarion Handbook* for 1958-9.

This Trespass differed in two ways from the earlier one on Kinder Scout. The most important difference was that whereas the Kinder Trespass was organised solely by the British Workers Sports Federation, without any effort being made to involve the Manchester Ramblers' Federation which, as we have seen, condemned it, the Abbey Brook Trespass emerged out of an official meeting of the Sheffield Ramblers' Federation. On the day of the actual trespass, this was an important factor. G.H.B. Ward was in the chair at the Ramblers' Federation meeting, attended by fifty representatives of rambling clubs, where the proposition was made. Opinions vary as to the attitude he took. A minority say he was totally opposed. The majority view is

24   Abbey Brook in the Derwent Valley, scene of the second mass trespass in September 1932.

that he was not against it, but would not himself back it, because it would place in jeopardy his job as a conciliation officer at the Ministry of Labour. In consequence he proposed that representatives of those clubs who were in favour — and this was a majority of those present — should meet separately and organise the trespass. This view of Ward's attitude is confirmed by the meeting he had before the event with the leaders of the Mass Trespass. At this meeting he outlined the law of trespass and explained why the Duke of Norfolk's Road was a right of way. Mr Revill, chairman of the Organising Committee, says that G.H.B. Ward wished them well at the end of the meeting.

Representatives from the Woodcraft Folk, the Onward, Pack, Brightside Independent Labour Party, Spartacus (set up by the Sheffield Young Communist League), Independent Labour Party Guild of Youth, Sheffield Education Settlement, Halcyon, Clarion Co-operative Ramblers, Good Companions, Holiday Fellowship (the latter two clubs withdrew from the struggle) met and organised the trespass. The committee numbered around twenty.

The sun was shining on the September day of the second Mass Trespass. Some 200 ramblers alighted from the tramcars at the Sheffield surburban termini of Malin Bridge and Middlewood. In a cheerful yet determined mood, well aware after the Kinder battle and gaol sentences of the reception which awaited them on Britain's most prolific grouse moor, they set off on the 3½-mile walk to the start of the trespass. This was, appropriately enough, the point where Bar Dike — a ten-foot deep, 350-yard trench, constructed by our early ancestors as a defensive earth work, joined Mortimer's Road, where the Duke of Norfolk's Road started. Since the earliest days, as recorded in the Sheffield *Clarion Handbook* of 1914, ramblers had been violently and quite illegally ejected from the track, which had prompted Ward to rummage through old records, also interviewing old inhabitants of the nearby hamlets and villages of Wiggtwizzle and Bradfield, seeking to prove it as an established right of way. Ward established that the public road[3] was legalised by the Ecclesfield Tithes and Enclosure Act of 1811, and was concluded in 1826, being sworn at the Tontine Inn, Sheffield. The road, crudely constructed of stone, went into the moorland but was never finished, continuing as a footpath and occasional bridleway to terminate at the outhouse of Abbey Grange Cottages in the Derwent Valley. When, prior to the Dissolution, the land belonged to a monastery, and up to the time of the enclosure, it was a horse and foot way. Viscount Fitzalan Howard, with whom Ward discussed the matter in 1925, refused to concede the right of way, which was only finally acknowledged in November 1955 by the West Riding County Council after the 1949 Act.[4]

The first sign of the formidable opposition the trespassers were to meet was a keeper perched on a nearby rock, who shouted an ineffectual 'keep off, you are not allowed to go on there', and then retreated, mounting his bicycle and furiously pedalling along the track shouting warnings to other posted look-outs. As the army of ramblers in orderly fashion stepped out along the moorland right of way, no serious resistance was encountered until they reached a point overlooking Abbey Brook. Here a force of some hundred or so gamekeepers, regular and temporary, armed with pick shafts (The Woodcraft Folk log book records 'pit props') and a few police, including an inspector, met the ramblers in a head-on clash. A scuffle ensued, as the cudgel-wielding keepers rained blows on the heads and shoulders of the ramblers. Fearing serious injury, the police advised the keepers to aim for the legs, with the result that many a rambler had bruised legs before the day was out.

After the first gamekeepers' assault was rebuffed and they regrouped for another attack, it became obvious to the ramblers' leaders that a serious situation might arise. The leaders instructed the ramblers to sit down and get out sandwiches and flasks, while they discussed the next steps. Having achieved their object of walking along the 'forbidden' right of way, the leaders recommended an about-turn. Most of the ramblers agreed, but a dozen including the author (then a youngster of 19) did not agree and set out for Howshaw Tor, wholly trespass ground, to Bradfield Gate Head, and returned down Foulstone Delph.

On the three-mile return journey the infuriated gamekeepers, egged on by the Duke of Devonshire's head keeper, insistently demanded that the police make arrests. One Young Communist Leaguer, Arthur Newson, a marked man, swopped clothing and glasses with a fellow rambler. Yet the police did not want another Derby trial. They were well aware of the fury which the Kinder sentences had aroused, knowing only too well from which quarter the violence had come. They hadn't even a casualty who could be put

25 *Gamekeepers attacking ramblers during the Abbey Brook trespass.*

up as 'proof' of the ramblers' violence. In fact the only 'injury' which their side sustained was that of a policeman who, bending down to tie up his shoe lace, had been tipped over into the peat by one of the girl ramblers, much to everybody's amusement. They were also very much aware that G.H.B. Ward had thoroughly established the existence of a right of way. So it was with much relief that the Superintendent bid the ramblers a polite good day, as the start of the Duke of Norfolk's Road was eventually reached.

The second point of difference from the Kinder Trespass was the large force of gamekeepers, regulars and temporary, numbering over a hundred. What particularly incensed the keepers was their failure to stop the trespassers even setting foot on the track. Owing to poor 'intelligence work' they assembled at the wrong end of the track, that is the Derwent End, while the trespass started off from the Bar Dike end. To reach the Mass Trespass they were confronted with a two or three mile rather stiff, up-hill walk along a rough moorland track. However, it was the police who this time played it low key, there being less than half a dozen present, although there were unconfirmed reports of van loads held in reserve.

How did the ramblers feel after it all? Defeated? Not a bit! Despite the claims of the gamekeeper, the ramblers were far from depressed. As a log written by a 16-year-old Woodcrafter explains: 'neither have they defeated us. It was a day full of excitement and next time we want 1,000 not 200.'

This was not the end of the protests. On Sunday 16 October an intended trespass along Stanage Edge was stopped by mounted and foot police who had

26 Keepers and police assembled after the trespass on the Duke of Norfolk's Road.

Alsatians with them. Twice they had stopped a meeting taking place on Burbage Bridge — it eventually was held on a path leading from Burbage Bridge to Fox House near Longshaw without police interference and was addressed by the leader of the Woodcraft Folk, Basil Rawson. Earlier there had been protest meetings against the sentences on the Kinder victims, held at Jacob's Ladder where 100 were present.

A planned trespass on Froggatt Edge on 4 September never materialised, though the police and keepers were there in strength. The organisers realised the dangers to which those participating would be exposed along the rocky edge.

References to Chapter 5

1 Rothman B., An account of the Mass Trespass written at the request of the Rambler's Association.
2 *Daily Express,* 25 April 1932
3 *Clarion Handbook* 1958-9
4 Ibid, 1957-8

6   *After the Mass Trespasses*

The Mass Trespasses had aroused widespread support among the half-million ramblers, for the simple fifty-year old demand for unrestricted access to moors and mountains.

Frank Turton, from the earliest times a prominent figure in the open-air movement and a one-time secretary of the Sheffield Ramblers' Federation, who played a leading part from the earliest days in the YHA, claims that thousands of people went to view the scene of the Kinder confrontation. Whatever criticisms the tactic of publicly trespassing on a disputed right of way and uncultivated moorland had brought, after the prison sentences the *Clarion Handbook* could say: 'the whole of the Federations of the country were aroused by what had been described as a savage sentence and are now exerting every effort to obtain full support for the Bill.'[1] Both the Sheffield and the Manchester Federations vigorously protested to the government, demanding clemency, but Ramsay Macdonald, a self-avowed trespasser, was no more prepared to release Rothman and his friends, than he had earlier been prepared to make a reality of his forthright support for access.

The Winnats Pass demonstration at Castleton in that same year, 1932, had a record attendance of 10,000. Both the Manchester and Sheffield Mass Trespassers interrupted some of the speeches, and displayed a red banner calling for militant action to 'win access now'. Professor Joad at the 1935 Winnats Rally urged the 5,000 assembled ramblers to become more militant' (*Manchester Guardian* 1 July 1935). Later in his book *The Untutored Townsman's Invasion of the Country,* he records saying on that occasion 'I should tell you that if you want the moors free, you must free them for yourselves.' In the same book he writes, the Mass Trespassers were '. . . certainly not the kind of thing I conceived myself to be exhorting . . . when I bade them free the moors.' However he wrote this in 1945, ten years after his militant speech and thirteen years after the Mass Trespasses. Little wonder that the militant ramblers of Sheffield and Manchester numbered him at the time as one of their most distinguished supporters.

Even in the south support was beginning to develop. The London Federation had always been lukewarm about access, and refused to organise any public demonstration. But a new London club appeared on the scene, the Progressive Rambling Club, led by a vigorous London militant, Phillip Poole. This club seized the initiative, and organised a 1,000 strong demonstration on Leith Hill, Surrey, which was addressed by Tom Stephenson, Stanley Baron and Lewis Silkin, and was supported by the

27 *The ramblers' demonstration in the Winnats Pass, Castleton, in 1932 when 10,000 people attended.*

Camping Club and the Clarion Touring Club. This was the first time since the battle for the London Commons in the middle of the last century, that anything like this had occurred in the capital city.

Scotland, where the access fight originated, and which had never since those early days shown much inclination to do anything, organised rallies of Scottish ramblers demanding freedom for access.[2] It is no exaggeration to say that the leaders of the ramblers' movement were riding on the crest of a powerful wave, embracing most parts of the country. 'There is a tide in the affairs of men which, taken at the flood, leads on to fortune.' This surely was such a time, despite the reactionary charter of the government elected in 1935.

But unfortunately the leaders allowed themselves to be outmanoeuvred by Lawrence Chubb, secretary of the Commons Open Spaces and Footpath Preservation Society. He had no mass backing as had the ramblers' leaders, and was an inveterate opponent of the only worthwhile access — that is, 'Without let or hindrance'. Not that the leaders of the ramblers were fully aware, especially in the early stages, of Chubb's role, though some like G.H.B. Ward had misgivings right from the start. Opposition by the

75

Commons Open Spaces and Footpath Preservation Society and its kindred organisations, such as the Council for the Preservation of Rural England, was first publicly voiced in 1928. The *Manchester Ramblers' Federation Handbook* of 1929, reporting on the Leicester Conference, at which a great variety of sporting organisations were present, wrote that it refused to associate with the demand for the public right of access to uncultivated mountain and moorland.

A one-day conference organised by the Commons Open Spaces and Footpath Preservation Society on 13 October 1931, reversed this and supported access. Yet this in no way prevented Chubb from working against the demand which his own organisation in the last century had first fought for. Instead of struggling for access they saw the way forward through the 1925 Law of Property Act and the Right of Way Act 1932. Just how effective these measures were was demonstrated in the Rombalds Moor dispute of 1934.

This large grouse moor near Ilkley is situated close to the large industrial towns of the West Riding. It was visited by thousands of open-air enthusiasts, especially during the spring and summer months. The owner caused notices to be erected closing it for five months of the year, during the grouse nesting and shooting seasons. This caused a tremendous outcry from the rambling clubs of the West Riding; 10,000 signatures to a petition launched by the West Riding Federation were collected, most of them on the moor itself.

As a result a Public Inquiry was held in September 1934. One of the ramblers' witnesses at the inquiry was Mr Alfred Joe Brown of Wharfdale, vice-president of the West Riding Ramblers' Federation. He represented over 3,000 affiliated local ramblers and 35,000 active members elsewhere. To these must also be added 40,000 members of the YHA. He told the inquiry that within walking distance of this moor was a population of just over one million people, and the moor was an essential lone space for this densely populated area. One proposal of the draft orders suggested that people should not sing or shout on the moor. To that he took strong exception, 'I am surprised that the crime of singing on a moor falls under the same category as obscene language or behaving in an indecent manner . . . we certainly claim the right to sing on the moor when the spirit moves us, Burley Moor is part and parcel of Ilkley or Rombalds, and if there is any moor in England which ought to be free for Yorkshiremen, I submit it is this moor, which is famous as a traditional playground of Yorkshiremen the world over.'

The outcome of the inquiry was a ministerial order cutting the restriction period by one month, so that it lasted from 1 April to 20 June and 10 August to 15 September, also 'on any other day on which red flags shall be flown indicating that shooting is taking place.'[3] As Edwin Royce pointed out, this was 'for sixty-five days' as a maximum in the six months from 1 April to 30 September, these being the best months of the year, including two or three Bank Holiday weekends when people want to enjoy the countryside. Little wonder that the West Riding Federation, in the words of its secretary, was now second to none in urging the needs for an Access Bill.

What remaining illusions the ramblers' leaders might have had should have been swept away following Chubb's speech to the Manchester Luncheon Club on 3 December 1934. He attacked the principle of access, declaring it would never be passed into law in their lifetime. These measures he said failed to take into account the fine old English attribute of 'fair play to both sides'. This aroused bitter denunciation from the leading figures in the northern movement. The Sheffield Federation protested against Chubb's attack on access; Royce in a satirical article declared 'fair play in the Peak — what mocking laughter would echo from the cliffs in the Winnats if that statement was made there . . . thrice have we fought to keep Doctor's Gate, first in 1909 to 1911, again in 1922 and, finally we trust, in 1925.' He also referred to '. . . two well known paths across Peakland moors to which the public is denied access: Alport Castle Route and the Duke of Norfolk's Road. They are rights of way typical of scores. What we have we have kept by vigilance and determination.'[4] In a letter to the *Manchester Guardian* he contrasted Chubb's and the Commons Society 's attitude with that of the early days. 'Now the society has become virtually an umpire between the landowners and the public.' Chubb, however, was no umpire when it came to the sentences passed on the Kinder Trespassers. He quite unashamedly aligned himself with the voice of the landowners. *The Field* published a letter from him on 4 June 1932, declaring that the action of the hikers was clearly indefensible. This attitude can also be seen in a letter Chubb wrote to George Mitchell, Secretary of the Ramblers' Association, the day after the Kinder Trespass, condemning it as a peculiar, stupid and mischievous business. He felt that those arrested should rightly face the consequences of their foolishness. Yet this letter revealed more than anything else his political prejudice, for it went on to state that he believed the Lancashire District of the Workers' Sport Federation was '. . . supported from Russia'! He was not, however, able to reveal his source for this information.[5]

During these years of what Ward had described as 'farcical' negotiations, reports had appeared in the press stating that a few paths were to be opened for a limited period each year on the Devonshire estates, a concession that both the Sheffield and Manchester Federations considered useless. In fact the Manchester Federation refused to take part in any further negotiations for this limited object.[6] The only concession wrung out of the Duke, was the removal of the 'No Road' notices on the West End to Alport Castles Farm bridle road in the Upper Derwent Valley, which were erected in 1923 to stop the Clarion Ramblers. Little wonder Ward considered the negotiations a waste of time and money, especially when attempts were being made to close down other tracks. One was at the back of Chatsworth House, the home of the Duke of Devonshire, which the Clarion Ramblers had traversed uninterruptedly for thirty years. Iron railings were also being erected to enclose the Moscar grouse moor, near Ladybower[7], and much of this is still intact.

In 1935 two discussions were held with the British Water Works Authority. They proved no more successful than did those with the grouse moor owners, and consequently the ramblers' representative proposed they should be dropped. This charade of negotiations was completely in line with the increasing intensity of the attack made by the grouse moor owners on the very concept of access. In 1932 *The Field* published an article by the Duke of Atholl, who according to *The Acreocracy of Perthshire* owned 140,000 acres, practically all deer forests.[8] He described the Access to Mountains Bill as a crank's measure, which would injure farming, sport, and rateable values. He also claimed it would injure sheep, eliminate game birds, and adversely affect rates. It has earlier been shown how extensive grouse rearing has resulted in a drastic decline in sheep, and as for rates, no less an authority than Stapleton has stated that the rates paid by Scottish Highlands were worth only 4d per acre as against 4s 4d for the rest of Scotland.[9] Any district, he wrote, which depended on sport for the major part of its rates would be in a sorry plight. A similar situation existed in England. The Duke went on to claim that there was not the slightest desire on the part of the general public to go on these hills. This was certainly not true of Scotland, for why were the Scottish landowners urging the Secretary of State for Scotland to alter the Trespass Law, so that persons found trespassing should be subject to a fine in addition to being liable to compensation for damage?[10]

One of the most oft repeated objections to public access had been the increased danger of vandalism and fire risk. No users of the countryside have done more than the organised ramblers not merely to condemn such acts, whether committed wantonly or carelessly, but actively to stop them. The purchase of Longshaw Estate near Grindleford in the Peak for the National Trust, some 1,000 acres in extent, half of which is woodland and half moorland, is a living example. It cost a total of £21,400, raised by public subscription, often in small amounts, by ramblers on the estate during the 1930 slump. A scheme of voluntary wardens, the first in the country, drawn mainly from the rambling clubs, was launched under the leadership of Phil Barnes. It is to their credit that no major fire has ever occurred since public access became possible, yet there are over five miles of footpath through the estate.

The Creech Jones Bill   The sorry story of Creech Jones' Access Bill shows that the landowners had not had any change of heart between 1932 and 1939. The most disastrous of all the negotiations were those surrounding the Access Bills of 1937 and 1938.[11] Mention has already been made of the fate which the 1931 Bill, sponsored by Ellen Wilkinson and others, had suffered at the hands of Ramsay Macdonald. Prior to this there had been five attempts since the end of World War I to get Access Bills through the House of Commons. All had failed. No one had opposed them — they had simply been ignored.

Both the Geoffrey Mander Bill of 1937, and the Creech Jones Bill of 1938, were similar to the original Bill introduced half a century earlier. In broad terms they sought to concede the right of public access to uncultivated mountains and moorlands for the purposes of recreational, artistic and scientific study, and providing no damage was done, there would be no action for trespass. The Creech Jones Bill did receive an unopposed second reading, which had not happened since the Trevelyan Bill of 1908. Naturally it aroused feelings of joy amongst many ramblers, especially when they saw the support the measure received from the press. Even Tory journals such as the *Spectator* urged the National Government to back it without a moment's hesitation. Even though some of the leading figures in the rambling movement were sceptical as to what exactly an 'agreed' measure would bring, the majority were jubilant, believing that the hopes and activities of over half a century were going to be realised. In order to mobilise all possible support for the Bill, the Access Sub-committee of the Ramblers' Association sent a letter to all MPs asking for their backing, and published a pamphlet for wide sale. The West Riding Federation launched a fighting fund. The Sheffield Federation widely distributed printed post-cards which were signed and posted in considerable number to MPs. The Executive Committee of the Youth Hostels Association also gave its support to the Bill.

Little did the leaders of the ramblers know the power which the Bill's opponents wielded in the affairs of state. Using Chubb, secretary of the Commons Open Spaces and Footpaths Preservation Society as a most willing tool, and other amenity organisations closely allied with his committee, they succeeded in emasculating a Bill which would have given access to all uncultivated land into an Act which, in the words of Chuter Ede MP, a member of the Cabinet in Attlee's first post-war Government 'was something which the landowners of the eighteenth century would not have dared given themselves.'[12] This was the infamous Trespass Clause, 'which would make it a criminal offence merely to be on wild moorland without causing any damage'. Trespass was made an offence in the reign of George II but was subsequently repealed.

The Trespass Clause was not in the original Creech Jones Bill. First mention of it was in the first draft of a proposed amended Bill sent to George Mitchell, secretary of the Ramblers' Association, with a covering letter from Chubb inviting them to appoint delegates to a conference to be held on 13 January 1939 to consider this amended version so that 'the Commons Open Spaces and Footpath Preservation Society may be acquainted with their views before meeting the representatives of the Landowners Association during the following week. . . .' At this conference the Trespass Clause aroused such opposition from the Ramblers' Association that Chubb promised the Bill would be redrafted and presented to a further conference which was held on 10 February. At this conference the principle of access to all uncultivated land was removed and in its place put an elaborate arrangement for obtaining limited access to specified areas, a procedure since incorporated in all subsequent legislation. The Ramblers' Association delegates reluctantly agreed to this change because no mention was made of the hated Trespass Clause. G.H.B. Ward writing in the *Clarion Handbook* 1940-1 said:

> In this draft there was no clause which could be construed as affecting the common law of trespass, therefore the matter was not raised . . . if it had been known that the objectionable trespass clause was to be re-introduced the delegates would have rejected the scheme *in toto*. Early in March yet another Draft Bill — issued by the Commons Society(?) — included several new and objectionable features which had not been discussed OR EVEN SEEN, by the Ramblers delegates.

When the Bill became an Act it contained in addition to the Trespass Clause fourteen other different offences for which an offender could be fined from £2 to £5. It also gave to the gamekeeper the legal right to demand names and addresses, and anyone failing to do so could be fined £5.

As we have seen earlier, trespass without damage had not been an offence for centuries, for as Sir Robert Hunter, one of the founders of the Commons Society, has said, 'When no damage can be done, and the owners' legitimate privacy cannot be intruded upon by an entry upon the lands, there is no longer any reason for considering such an entry to be trespass.'[13]

This unfortunate position can only be put down to Chubb who, based on Ward's evidence, deceived the majority of the ramblers' leaders, an action which according to Stanley Baron writing in *Out of Doors* (May-June 1948), 'was a cause of grief he never quite got over', and to the personal egotism of Creech Jones, who Tom Stephenson claims, became obsessed with piloting his Bill through Parliament no matter what concessions he had to make.[14] Far from being considered the heroic figure among the ramblers which his seconder for the Bill prophesied, he became the most reviled. At a public meeting in the Geographical Hall, held in Manchester, so great was the feeling against him that he was almost shouted down.[15]

Even before Creech Jones introduced his Bill into the House, Chubb, the National Trust, and the Council for the Preservation of Rural England, were lobbying Geoffrey Mander MP, who was sponsoring an earlier measure, which caused Royce to write that 'compromise is a hateful thing to many of us and to some will smack of treachery.'[16] Chubb was opposed to access, for in January 1933 he had written to George Mitchell, 'We do not think that the Access to Mountains Bill can be wholeheartedly supported in as much it is in some respects tantamount to confiscation. . . . Later he went on to explain:

If this [ie access to moorlands] can be done by agreement, or by the payment of compensation to the landowner, no one would be likely to object. But it is pointed out by the owners, that to throw open to the multitude, areas bought and strictly maintained for sport, would have the effect of destroying their economic value . . . and we are bound to accept the views of the best friend of the open-air movement in Parliament, that there is no prospect whatever of the Access to the Mountains Bill being passed into law, within any time that can be seen . . . an equitable and amicable solution has to be found . . . by the grant to responsible Local Authorities or voluntary organisations, of permissive ways, under terms which will ensure that members of recognised rambling clubs and allied bodies of pedestrians, if not the general public, shall be allowed to pass from point to point except during the actual shooting season.[17]

An elitist proposition if ever there was one! The rambler had already had a foretaste of this on Rombalds moor, which had aroused widespread protest.

Based on Chubb's approach, the Duke of Devonshire made proposals to the Sheffield and Manchester Federations, which they rejected. The proposals of the landowners and Chubb were a far cry from the straightforward access principle upon which the Bryce Bills were based, and events in the Peak, Ilkley Moor and on the Cairngorms during the 1950s, when these grouse moors became freely walked over by the rambler, have shown that 'bags' are as big as ever they were when access was denied.

This about-face happened following the conference called by the Commons Open Spaces and Footpath Preservation Society and the CPRE on October 22 1937. The outcome of this was the setting up of a joint committee 'to consider in what ways the bill can be amended without sacrifice of essentials, so as to secure a reasonable chance of it becoming law'.[18] Chubb opened up negotiations with the landowners, government departments and MPs concerned.

Yet even after this it was not until March that the ramblers saw this Bill for what it was — a 'landowners' protection bill', not a Ramblers' Charter. In fact the only good thing about it was that it did not apply to Scotland. Unfortunately, as Phil Barnes observed, it had taken a long time to convince the others that the ramblers should publicly oppose this Bill. As late as February 21 the National Executive Committee of the ramblers were still supporting the Bill[19], as they did in a big rally attended by 800 people, held at the Friends Meeting House, Euston Road, London, and addressed by Hugh Dalton (Labour), Graham White (Liberal), Dr E.A. Baker and Stephen Morton. Morton has said that at this meeting he was prevailed upon by Chubb and Dalton not to be too controversial, as it might endanger the negotiations. Tom Stephenson remonstrated with Morton for removing the offending portions of his speech. In fact Stephenson had much earlier suspected that a sell-out was being prepared. Morton has since regretted that he heeded Chubb's and Dalton's pressure. As Tom Stephenson has written, 'The ramblers joy over his success was short-lived, for the Bill was mutilated in Committee as to emerge worthless to ramblers.'

At the Annual General Meeting of the Ramblers' Association held on 19 March 1939 a resolution condemning the Bill was carried. The Sheffield Federation organised a large and enthusiastic protest meeting and a similar protest meeting was organised in Liverpool. Unfortunately, their full realisation of the shameful way they had been deceived was too late to alter the course of events. On April 25 the Bill completed its second reading in the House of Lords without a division. The grouse moor owners and shooting syndicates were more than pleased with the Trespass clause — and well they might be. Under the guise of free public access to moors and mountains they had got a punitive measure, which could make every harmless rambler a criminal.

Seldom in the chequered history of parliamentary double dealing, has democracy been so blatantly abused. Little wonder that Edwin Royce, a man who had worked so hard and long for the cause of access, was so depressed that when he knew his end was approaching he proposed in a letter to Tom Stephenson 'that he would trespass persistently on Kinder Scout until an injunction was obtained against him, and that he should then continue trespassing with the inevitable consequence of being sent to gaol. His imprisonment, he thought, might give some publicity to the 'access' position and help forward the demand for new legislation.'[20]

Is there any wonder that these acts of surrender should have resulted in the once powerful movement of support being frittered away? Eight years earlier the Mass Trespass leaders had been told that militancy did not pay. Their public acts of defiance at a time when responsible negotiations with the landowners were beginning were said to have set the movement back twenty years. But had they? During the whole of the so-called negotiations, 'the representatives of the Ramblers' Federation have never met in conference the representatives of the landowners.'[21] Chubb acted as a go-between, and was privy to the proposals, which were often never revealed to the ramblers' leaders. In no sense can they be regarded as genuine negotiations; the ramblers were treated worse than a defeated enemy. G.H.B. Ward admitted this when he wrote, 'The Communist may ask for access . . . but he appears to have the laugh at this poor Act.'[22]

It was not militancy that had failed, but lack of it. This is demonstrated by what happened in at least one respect on the Sheffield side of the Peak. The Labour-controlled Sheffield City Council during the mid-thirties granted increased access to Burbage Moors, terminating the shooting of grouse on these, and Houndkirk Moors. Even a 'sufferance' path over Win Hill in the Hope Valley was secured, and the right of way over Derwent Edge very near to the scene of the Abbey Brook Mass Trespass was conceded.

No such genuine concessions were secured in the area covered by the Manchester Federations. The Manchester Corporation Waterworks Committee, because of its refusal to instal modern filtration techniques, was numbered amongst the worst in the country. The position in the Forest of Bowland was intolerable. It was not until the post-war years that any progress was made, and even then public demonstrations were needed. Can the difference be due to the more friendly attitude of the Sheffield Ramblers' Federation to the Mass Trespassers than was the case with Manchester? I suggest that this is a very feasible explanation.

Not that the leaders of the Mass Trespasses, which so electrified the rambling world, can escape the responsibility for the debacle. They withdrew from the struggle as it was entering its most critical phase, and when support for their militant policies was increasing among the ever-growing movement of ramblers. Bernard Rothman has accepted this. In an interview given anonymously he agreed that they made plenty of mistakes: 'The big one was of course that we entirely ignored the organised ramblers and in fact considerably antagonised them by our reference to them in our publicity.'[23]

References to Chapter 6

1 *Clarion Handbook*, 1933-4
2 *Ramblers' Journal*, National Council of Ramblers' Federations (1936)
3 *Ramblers' Federation Handbook*, 1936
4 *Ramblers' Journal*, March 1935
5 Rickwood, P.W., *Public Enjoyment of Open Countryside in England and Wales 1919-1939*, (Unpublished PhD Thesis, Faculty of Social Sciences, University of Leicester 1973), p235

6 *Ramblers' Federation Handbook*, 1938
7 *Clarion Handbook*, 1935-6
8 *The Acreocracy of Perthshire*, Perth and Kinross Fabian Society, p9
9 *Out of Doors*, June 1938
10 *Ramblers' Journal*, September 1933
11 *Clarion Handbook*, 1939-40
12 Stephenson, T., *The Campaign for Countryside Legislation*, (1969), P26
13 *Ramblers' News*, (The Magazine of the Ramblers' Association), Summer 1958
14 Rickwood, P.W., *op cit*, p282
15 *25 Milestones, (op cit*, Chapter 4)
16 *Ramblers' Federation Handbook*, 1938
17 Ibid, 1934
18 Ibid, 1938
19 Rickwood, P.W., *op cit*, p291
20 *Out of Doors*, Spring 1947
21 *Memorandum on the Amended Bill*, issued by the Ramblers' Association, 1938
22 *Clarion Handbook*, 1941-2
23 *The Progressive Rambler*, 1940, no70

7 The Post War Years

The post 1939-45 war years have been portrayed as the period when all the dreams and long-fought for struggles for access were achieved. Some access at a price has undoubtedly been won, but it is very small in comparison both with the demands of the early campaigners, and with the vast areas of uncultivated land. It is certainly inadequate to meet the growing need of all those who are seeking recreational facilities on what remains of Britain's wild country. To secure it needed continuing pressure, and before the freedom to roam on Britain's hills is fully realised it may be necessary to resort to the kind of struggles which were such a feature of the Peak in the first forty years of this century.

It has continued ever since, because this simple demand was interpreted by landowners and owners of sporting rights as a· serious attack on the proprietorial rights of ownership and pursuits. Yet every prominent figure in the long struggle for access has always denied that the conceding of this right would in any way militate against the rearing and shooting of game birds. Experience since the 1949 Act has abundantly demonstrated the correctness of this. It still remains a battle in many areas today, not because the leisure needs of landowners are at this stage incompatible with the existing outdoor recreational needs of the many, (whether this will always remain so is discussed later) but because the majority of the shooting fraternity still regard the land used for the pursuit of their sport as their exclusive legal right. They have only, in the post-war period, conceded legal public access because to have refused it might have resulted in a confrontation more serious than anything experienced in the first forty years of this century. Tom Stephenson in an interview recalls the memorandum he submitted to the Scott Committee in which he instances the Mass Trespasses of the early 1930s as the sort of thing that could occur again in the post-war period.

The 1939 Creech Jones Access to Mountains Act was condemned from all sides of the rambling movement. Few people had a good word for it. The Ramblers' Association memorandum declared that it gave no access to a yard of land. Stanley Baron writing in the *News Chronicle* used similar words: 'No Access anywhere, it merely provides cumbersome machinery for getting it sometime — somewhere — maybe.'[1] Dower in his oft-quoted report stated that 'No access rights whatever are secured by the Act.'

As we have seen it was the infamous Trespass Clause which aroused the greatest hostility amongst the ramblers, though the rest of the Act which finally emerged from consultations and committees 'was an elborate and entirely different fourteen page measure' from the original simple two-page measure which Creech Jones proposed.[2] Had this simple Bill reached the Statute Book, then the sixty-year-old demand voiced so eloquently by James Bryce in Parliament in 1892 would have been realised — the right of the people to go freely over the mountains of their own country.[3]

The Act was universally condemned and never operated, but by setting a pattern for negotiated access limited to specific areas, it marks a watershed in the parliamentary battle. For never again has parliament had before it a Bill which would restore the right to walk 'without let or hindrance' for purposes of air and exercise on *all* uncultivated land.

Instead of acceding to this basic desire the 1939 Act substituted a procedure whereby each separate area, in the words of the Ramblers' Association memorandum, had to be fought for and won with each owner. This is a retreat from the Law of Property Act of 1925 which gave the legal right of access for purposes of 'air and exercise' subject only to regulations to prevent abuse or damage to all urban commons — a principle first established in the last century by the people of London and the south in their struggles to prevent the enclosures of the commons. It also applied to Yorkshire's famous Ilkley Moor.

Although the ramblers were not happy at this abandonment of the basic principle of access after the introduction of the Trespass Clause, it was the machinery through which this piecemeal approach for access was to be negotiated which became their primary concern. Application for access had to be made by an owner, Local Authority or approved organisation. If there were any objections, a public inquiry had to be held, following which the Minister of Agriculture might make an order confirming access over all or part of the land; not only were all the general conditions, as laid down by the Act, applicable, but he could impose any other condition to protect the owner against any detriment. There were those in the leadership who were for trying to operate the Act, but when in April 1940 the Minister issued Statutory Rules and Orders governing the administration of the Act, it became obvious how unworkable it was.

Those applying for access were required to prepare six-inch maps, which were to be sent to everyone having an interest in the land, not just the owner. Before the holding of a public inquiry, the Minister may request the applicant to deposit a sum of money to meet the cost of the inquiry and of any expenses or fees incurred in the making of an order. The applicant had to erect and maintain notice boards on the land to which the order applied — G.H.B. Ward considered this may mean anything up to five hundred in the Peak. Little wonder the Ramblers' Association protested to the Minister against these further impositions. To have attempted to operate the Act would have bankrupted them.

It was the outbreak of the 1939-45 war which finally decided the Ramblers' Association not to apply for legal orders, as it would detract from the war effort. A letter to the press signed by the chairmen of eight Footpath Preservation Societies and Ramblers' Federations in the north of England explained why, with the outbreak of war, it would not be proper to use the machinery for access. In return they expressed the hope that many landowners would be patriotic enough to dedicate the new country and moorland paths to the use of the public, in return for the sacrifices which were now being made, 'and as some contribution to the cause of freedom in which landowners and public are united.'[4] It was all in vain: patriotism certainly motivated the ramblers, but not the landowners; they never responded. Little wonder the ramblers decided that when the young generation then in the Services returned they would 'start a new fight' for a new Act, in a better balanced House of Commons which even before the war started was expected at the next general election.[5] This was the predominant attitude of all those in the rambling movement, including G.H.B. Ward who declared, 'The Act is dead for the duration of this war, and afterwards it must be the basis upon which to erect a respectable mountain instead of this microscopic mole-hill.'[6] Yet it was by no means the end of the argument about whether to try and operate it. In fact, there developed around this issue the first most serious policy rift in the leadership of the rambling movement.

Among the British people, at war for the second time in the lives of many, there was an unmistakeable feeling that not again were they going to be cynically betrayed by the empty high-sounding pledges which had fallen so glibly from the lips of the 1914-18 leaders. If and when victory was won, they demanded something more than the wasted years of the lean and hungry thirties. This time they would walk and climb freely on the moors, glens and mountains of Britain's grouse lands and deer forests, without having to defend themselves from the abuse and violence of the gamekeepers.

The war-time government, well aware of this mood, set in motion plans to prepare for the post-war reconstruction, including the need to meet the demands of all who cherished the countryside and were determined they would secure the right to enjoy it to the full. The Scott Committee was set up early in October 1941, to consider the conditions which should govern building and constructional development in the countryside. The committee, however, stretched its terms of reference, and accepted evidence on the preservation and use of the countryside. To the Scott Committee, the Ramblers' Association submitted a lengthy memorandum, later published as a pamphlet. In addition to reviewing the proposals for the creation of National Parks embracing the wild and pastoral areas such as the Peak, Lake District and South Downs, it urged that the public should have the right to walk at will in the wilds, including water gathering grounds, coast and foreshores. The memorandum urged that in addition to numerous new footpaths, a number of long distance routes should be created, such as the Pennine Way, Offa's Dyke, the Pilgrims' Way, and the South Downs Route from Beachy Head to Winchester and on to Salisbury Plain.

The committee reported in August 1942; it endorsed the proposals of the Ramblers' Association declaring 'The precept that the countryside is the heritage of all involves the corollary that there must be facility for access to all.' It also endorsed the recording by Local Authorities on maps of all footpaths with a small footpath commission to investigate and give decisions on disputed cases; and the making of main hiker highways such as the Pennine Way and including the old coastguard paths.

In 1945 came probably the most famous of all the reports — the Dower Report on National Parks in England and Wales, which set out and agreed with 'the insistent claims of all ramblers' organisations and of the large and growing army of individual walkers . . . that the public shall have the right to wander at will over their whole extent, subject only to a minimum of regulations to prevent abuse, and to a minimum of excepted areas where such wandering would clearly be incompatible with some other publicly necessary use of the land.' The report made it quite clear, that this did not include grouse shooting, for in paragraph 45 it states, 'When the issue is seen as a broad question of principle — whether the recreational needs of the many should or should not outweigh the sporting pleasures of the few — there can be little doubt of the answer; that the walker should, and sooner or later will, be given freedom of access over grouse moors.' Regarding water gathering grounds, which Dower recognised presented a more difficult problem, he urged the appropriate treatment of the water, such as was done to the water drawn from the River Thames to supply London's domestic needs.

After the post-war General Election of 1945, which gave Labour the biggest majority it has ever had in the House of Commons, a public committee was appointed, known as the Hobhouse Committee, which stated, 'The freedom to wander over mountain, moorland and rough grazing, and other uncultivated land will be of the utmost importance.' In July 1946, the Access Sub-Committee was appointed to go more fully into the problem. It recommended that access should be given to all uncultivated land, whether mountain, moor, heath, down, cliff, beach or shore. The Ramblers' Association, not content with submitting its proposals to these committees, publicly campaigned for them. Following the 1945 General Election Lewis Silkin, who had long been in sympathy with the aims of the ramblers, was made Minister of Town and Country Planning. He had spoken, along with Tom Stephenson, at the 1,000 strong pre-war demonstration at Leigh Hill. He recalled Tom's retort at that meeting to Creech Jones — who in justification of his 1939 Bill claimed that it was the best obtainable, short of a minor social revolution. 'Why', said Tom, 'are we wasting our time on piffling legislation like this instead of striving for the minor social revolution?'

Recalling this speech upon assuming ministerial office, Silkin sent for Tom Stephenson, who by this time was press officer to Silkin's Ministry, enquiring what he could do. Whereupon Tom urged Silkin to meet a deputation from the Ramblers' Association saying, 'if you talk to them as you have talked to me, they will go away delighted.' And so they did, for following the meeting, which took place on 12 December 1945, a press statement was issued by the Ministry, which paid tribute to the great work of the Ramblers' Association, and quite precisely spelt out that 'There must be facilities for access to the wild uncultivated areas of Britain'[7] — the first such pledge that the ramblers had had since Labour formed the post-war administration. That Silkin's undertaking were no window-dressing was clearly shown by Hugh Dalton, Labour's Chancellor of the Exchequer. In his budget of April 1946, he set aside a sum of fifty million pounds which, he said, 'might be described as a nest egg, set aside, which could be used to finance some of the operations

28 G.H.B. Ward speaking at the 1946 ramblers' rally in Cave Dale, Castleton.

necessary, in order to give to the public permanent access to the National Parks.'

The ramblers now fully expected that a Bill would be introduced in time to become an Act within the lifetime of Labour's first period. They were somewhat alarmed when, though the legislation was practically ready, whispers reached them that Herbert Morrison, Lord President of the Council, who was responsible for the parliamentary programme, was for delaying the introduction of the Bill until the spring of 1950. As Tom Stephenson recalls: 'We saw the danger if the government went to the country before its term of office expired, the legislation would not reach the Statute Book.' Whereupon the Ramblers' Association launched its public campaign.

Leaflets and pamphlets were distributed, MPs inundated with letters, and a series of public meetings was held in Manchester, Bradford, Leeds, Newcastle and Liverpool. The famous pre-war demonstrations in the Peak, organised jointly by the Sheffield and Manchester area associations were restarted as early as 1946, the first, held in Cave Dale, Castleton, on 30 June, was attended by 5,000 ramblers. Public meetings were also held in

Birmingham and London. At the Birmingham meeting, on 11 March 1948, before an audience of 1,500 ramblers, Lewis Silkin declared, 'We are absolutely with you in the objectives which you have before you.' So committed was the government to the introduction of the necessary legislation that Silkin declared 'pressure is unnecessary'.[8] The Right Honourable Chuter Ede, a member of Labour's Cabinet, addressing 1,600 people in London's Kingsway Hall at a meeting on 12 February 1948 said: 'We in the government will be just as disappointed if legislation dealing with the Hobhouse Report does not find its way on to the Statute Book in the lifetime of the parliament.'[9]

Tom Stephenson still remained apprehensive and hit upon the novel, yet quite characteristic, idea of taking a number of prominent members of the Labour government on a three-day walking holiday at Whitsuntide 1948, on the Pennine Way between Middleton-in-Teesdale and the Roman Wall. Along with Tom were Hugh Dalton, who that year was President of the Ramblers' Association, MPs Barbara Castle, Arthur Blenkinsop, George Chetwynd, Geoffrey de Freitas and Fred Willey. At the end of the walk Hugh Dalton said,

> After renewing acquaintance with this beautiful part of the country I am sure that we must in the lifetime of the Parliament place on the Statute Book a great measure of liberation, freeing for the health and enjoyment of all our people, what for so long has been monopolised by a few. National Parks so long talked about must be brought into being. The law regarding rights of way must be clarified and strengthened to remove the bias in favour of the landlord, to prevent the public losing through sharp practice, or neglect, rights of way to which they are entitled. Subject always to full recognition of the needs of agriculture and forestry, the public should have free and unquestioned access to mountain and moorland and all the wilder parts of Britain.

However, and not for the first time, attempts were being made to delay the introduction of a Bill which would replace the much-criticised 1939 Creech Jones measure. Before the end of the war, G.H.B. Ward acting on the advice of Fred Marshall, MP for Sheffield Brightside, and J.S. Middleton, Secretary of the Labour Party, urged that efforts must be made to operate Acts of Parliament before they can be amended or replaced. Ward therefore proposed that the Ramblers' Association should ask the Local Authority 'to apply for a Public Access Order to Kinder Scout — or subscribe to our cost — or that we should apply for the order to this important moor in Derbyshire and test the Act.'[10] At a meeting held in Stephen Morton's office were Ward, Barnes and Royce with Stephenson in the Chair, and this proposal was rejected. It was later endorsed at the Longshaw conference of the Ramblers' Association by a two to one majority.

1 Rickwood, P.W., (see ref 5, Chapter 6), p335
2 Dower, John, *National Parks in England and Wales* (HMSO cmd 6628, 1945), para 51
3 Rickwood, P.W., *op cit*, p249
4 *Clarion Handbook*, 1940-1
5 *Ramblers' Journal*, Winter 1938-9
6 *Clarion Handbook*, 1941-2
7 *Rucksack*, October 1966
8 *Out of Doors*, May-June 1948
9 Stephenson, T., (see ref 12, Chapter 6), p18
10 *Clarion Handbook*, 1945-6

8 The National Parks and Access to the Countryside Act 1949

The 1949 National Parks and Access to the Countryside Act was hailed by the government as 'the first time in English history an Act has been passed by parliament with the object of setting out in a workable form a comprehensive charter of rights for all lovers of the open air.'[1] Now, thirty years on, it is possible to judge how justified is this most forthright of claims. At the heart of the Ramblers' Charter, the earliest and certainly the most important of all demands is for the restoration of the right to walk 'without let or hindrance' for the purpose of air and exercise on Britain's uncultivated land. As Hobhouse noted, it was only within the last one hundred years that it had been 'severely restricted', as 'expensive forms of shooting and stalking were developed.' Therefore it was the restoration of an ancient right, not the demand of a new one, for which the ramblers from their earliest days had been struggling. Like its predecessor this Act did not automatically concede it. Whether it provided a 'workable form' for achieving this much fought for end, we shall examine in the course of this chapter.

As we have seen, ten years earlier the Creech Jones Act had been roundly condemned by ramblers, precisely because of its failure to end this abuse of 'freedom' which Stanley Baron of the *News Chronicle*, in the tradition of all great English radicals, claimed: 'damned it as a means of providing true liberty.'[2] All the officially appointed government committees charged with the task of preparing for post-war Britain had without equivocation endorsed this original demand of freedom of access for the rambler.

Dower in his report had declared that there was 'a strong case... to confer public rights of access over *all* uncultivated land (suitably defined) by direct and immediately operative measures.'[3] Nor was there lack of precedents. It was already part of the Law of Property Act 1925, and applied to all urban commons.

The Hobhouse Report stated: 'we consider that in National Parks public access as of right should be established over all suitable land.'[4] A Footpath and Access to the Countryside sub-committee was set up to devise a scheme whereby this could be achieved. This it set out in paragraph 159 of its report which proposed a procedure for the issuing of statutory maps which, after considering objections and holding, if necessary, public inquiries, should define land available for the right of public access for 'Air and pedestrian exercise.'[5] Despite being a supporter of access, Lewis Silkin, on assuming office, was reluctant to implement this. 'After all', he said, 'in the existing state of society and the law, a person's land is his land. I think it is wrong to give the public an automatic right to go over all private land of a certain character.'

Little wonder such a statement, contrary to everything he had said earlier, amazed many of his colleagues and dismayed the ramblers who declared: 'This falls far short of the Association's ideal of the general right of access and will inevitably cause complication and confusion and delay.'[6]

Then why this sudden about-face? The answer is given in a circular sent to Local Authorities on 23 October 1950. It suggested that, 'Where the proportion of open country over which some kind of access is available is adequate for the needs of the whole area that it might reasonably be regarded as serving, no further action is necessary.' The circular also urged Local Authorities not to disturb without good reason, 'friendly understanding or mutual indifference between landowners and the public . . . unless and until either party show such a reason.' But as the *Ramblers' News* wrote, 'this is to give away the whole case for access . . . wild country is meant for walking on freely, and apart from some quite exceptional consideration the right should be as near automatic as makes no difference. Anything less stinks in our nostrils . . .'[7] The Commons Open Spaces and Footpath Preservation Society had no such worries; drawing attention in the April 1956 number of its journal to the few access agreements outside of the Peak, it writes: 'This need not be cause for concern, as long as the public enjoy freedom to wander on uncultivated land by courtesy and do not abuse the privilege.'

Yet all the evidence accumulated over fifty years of struggle had conclusively shown that such landowners were in a minority. To frame an Act, especially after the 1939 experience on such exceptions, was to fly in the face of all the long and bitter struggles which had taken place.

Having rejected this elementary demand, the Act fell back on the piecemeal approach of the discredited Creech Jones Act, with this important difference. Whereas the 1939 Act had placed the burden of negotiating access on the shoulders of the ramblers' organisations, the 1949 Act transferred this responsibility, with the exception of the Peak and the Lake District, to the Local Authorities in whose administrative areas much disputed and desirable tramping and climbing country was situated. In the Peak the Act created a separate authority, with full powers, staff, and money obtainable by precept to operate. In the Lakes the amount of precept was limited to £7,500. The Act also, for the first time and with strict limiting qualifications, conceded the right of compensation for proven damage which public access may cause. Its most important innovation, which may well prove to be its most historic, was the official stamp it gave to wardening, the most effective measure yet devised to prevent wanton and thoughtless damage by the public to our most precious heritage, the countryside. It is hoped the time is not too far distant, when all who live, work and visit it, acquire the same concern as do the wardens for its preservation.

It is outside the scope of this book to examine how far the 1949 Act has succeeded in satisfying the advocates of National Parks — a demand which stretches back further than that for access. Important as National Parks are, the campaign for them has never reached such levels of confrontation as has happened with regard to access. Nevertheless much more has been achieved. There are ten National Parks in England and Wales all with powers to control the use to which land can be put, whereas the amount of legal public access is pitifully small: 91,215 acres in 1975 which is 1.9 per cent of rough grazing land in England and Wales. To this may be added two further amounts. Land owned by the National Trust amounting to 197,720 acres (Benson Report) though Thomson and Whitley in their paper 'The Economics of Public Access in the Countryside' (University of Newcastle upon Tyne) state this is '. . . a somewhat vague estimate, including a large area of *de facto* access land.' Also land to which the public have access for 'air and exercise' under the Law of Property Act 1925 amounting to 400,000 acres of common land, (*Our Common Heritage*, published by the Commons Open Spaces and Footpath Preservation Society). Adding these three amounts together increases the amount of access land to 4.8 per cent.

There are those who consider land to which *de facto* access exists should also be added. However the Commons Open Spaces and Footpath Preservation Society in their journal of Summer 1978 write 'The extent to which *de facto* access exists over the remaining 1,100,000 acres of common land is a matter for speculation.' A point made by Dower when he wrote 'an undefined, unreliable and irregular custom or privilege of access no longer meets the need either of walkers . . . or of farmers and owners.'

Nevertheless the National Parks as such have never satisfied the demands of their advocates, and today their existence is in as great jeopardy as ever it was. As most of the open country was within the ten National Parks boundaries, it was natural that there should be an intimate link between access and the Parks. Qualification for receiving the 75 per cent government grant for costs incurred by access agreements was subject to the area being within a National Park boundary. This was a qualification seized on by some Authorities as an excuse to do nothing, although later legislation has removed this limiting factor.

Apart from the failure to grant immediate access, the other great weakness of the Act was its non-application to Scotland — surely a mockery to James Bryce, whose pioneering zeal had launched access to mountains on its long, tedious legislative career. Even though this has since been remedied by the Countryside (Scotland) Act 1967, which created the Scottish Countryside Commission, it has still to register its first large-scale access agreement.

How successful has the Act been in operating its workable provisions? Dower estimated that there were 12,000 square miles of open country, about one-fifth the land area in England and Wales. If Scotland is added, and since the 1967 Act it should be included, the proportion is very much higher, comprising over one-third of the land area of Great Britain. Dower deducted land which, though 'wild enough, is insufficiently beautiful.' He also excluded isolated patches, land used for large-scale afforestation, quarrying, mining, and military ranges. 'But', he goes on, 'when all necessary deductions have been made . . . there still remains . . . some eight thousand square miles in England and Wales.' Up to 1975 public access under part 5 of the 1949 Act has been secured to 91,215 acres.[8] A pitiful achievement, and even if this rate of progress is maintained it will be many decades before the pioneers' original goal becomes a reality. Yet as we move into the final years of the twentieth century, it is less the vindication of what those far-sighted pioneering spirits battled for, than the need to cope with the increasing leisure needs of a rising population, by which the Act should be judged.

It is precisely this which is the greatest weakness of all in the 1949 Act; it legislated for the past not the future. Evidence to the House of Lords Committee on Sport and Leisure has drawn attention to this, and expressed concern at a recurrence of the pre-1939 confrontations. So they should, for built into the Act was the need to organise militant actions as the only way of obtaining public access from unwilling owners. Such has been the twenty-two years' experience of its operation, which subsequent Acts have done nothing to change. How true this is will be demonstrated by the struggles which have taken place in the West Riding and the Forest of Bowland, and also in the way the Act was framed.

It was Mr Brunt, Deputy Director and Planning Officer of the Peak Park Planning Board,[9] giving evidence to the House of Lords Committee on Sport and Leisure, who said that part 5 of the 1949 Act was written specifically for the Peak District. He recalled that in the inter-war period there were

> impediments, or what we might call conflicts or restraints. One of the conflicts was, on the one hand the outdoor movement of ramblers and climbers who felt they had a right to walk on the open, wild remote areas of the Peak District, but on the other hand, this land was in use; it had a value, and the farmers, gamekeepers, the landowners and the shooters had their point of view. I think the access provisions of the National Parks and Access to the Countryside Act were to provide power to deal with this situation. I do not think quite the same situation arose at that time in any other part of the country, but I think it is developing now.

As we have seen, this conflict reached its zenith in the Mass Trespasses of 1932; an event not unnoticed by the Access Sub-committee. In the post-war world of 1945, following the victory over Hitler, it was inconceivable that the struggle for the right to walk freely over the grouse moors of the Peak would not be taken up with renewed vigour. This is why not only did the 1949 Act treat as an exception the 542 square miles of the Peak, but so did the grouse-moor owners, calculating that if, via the Act, they conceded access in the Peak, they would be better able to maintain the privacy of the grouse moors elsewhere. Nor were they unmindful of Dower's very radical proposal of the special nature of the northern part of the Peak, especially Kinder Scout and Bleaklow, which they said 'may call for a more drastic solution'. This was to buy out the shooting values — plus the freehold, where privately owned — over a wide area, and to re-let the shooting subject to a prior public right of full regulated access.[10] The estimated cost for the control of 20,000 acres of Peak Moorland was £218,000. The acquisition of easements over the moors was estimated to cost £150,000.[11]

As we have already noted, the Peak Park Planning Board was the only one of its kind set up by the Act and this has been regarded by many as justification for the inter-war struggles for access. It is insufficiently appreciated that a landowner, even in the Peak, if he were so minded, could have considerably thwarted the purposes of the Act by dragging out interminably the negotiations and so preventing the Minister from approving an Access Order. The Act provided that where the negotiations failed the Public Authority could issue an order, but for this to become operative it would need the Minister's consent. No such order was ever made in the Peak although they were often threatened. In fact the only serious opposition which faced the Peak Planning Board was from a group of farmers.

This it may be thought is evidence of a change of heart by the grouse-moor owners, particularly the Duke of Devonshire, one of Britain's biggest and longest established landowners; for though to him goes the credit for signing one of the first access agreements, on Kinder Scout, it was he who resisted demands for access onto his Barden Moor in West Yorkshire. This, I suggest, is evidence that by conceding access in the Peak he calculated he would be in a stronger position to retain his privileges in West Yorkshire. Yet, if this surmise is correct it was in vain, for although he still retains some private shooting, he gave way to pressure from the ramblers of West Yorkshire.

This is the explanation for the Act's success in the Peak. The major credit rightly belongs to the unsung heroes of the northern ramblers and bog-trotters, who since the last century have campaigned for access. Not that there is access to all the grouse moors of the Peak; one of Britain's earliest and most prolific grouse moors, Broomhead, has still to be legally opened to access.

References to Chapter 8

1 *National Parks and Access to the Countryside*, Ministry of Town and Country Planning and Central Office of Information, p16
2 *News Chronicle*, 18 July 1939
3 Dower, John, (see ref 2, Chapter 7), para 52
4 *Report of the National Parks Committee, England and Wales*, (HMSO cmd 7121, 1947), para 291
5 *Report of the Committee on Footpaths and Access to the Countryside*, (HMSO cmd 7207, 1947), para 291
6 *Ramblers' News*, Spring 1949
7 Ibid, Winter 1950-51
8 Gibbs, R.S. and Whitby, M.C., *Local Authority Expenditure on Access Land*, (Agricultural Adjustment Unit, University of Newcastle upon Tyne), Appendix iii
9 *Second Report from the Select Committee of the House of Lords on Sport and Leisure*, para 603
10 Dower, John, *op cit*, para 46
11 Rickwood, P.W., (see ref 5, Chapter 6), p39

9 Access in the Peak and the West Riding of Yorkshire

The Peak 48,817 acres (76 square miles) of moors and mountains to which the public have legal access is in the Peak. This represents 56 per cent of all access land in Britain. This is about a third of the open country within the Peak National Park boundaries — approximately 236 square miles.[1] Bearing in mind the cumbersome machinery set up by the Act, and the ministerial lack of enthusiasm, amounting at times to actual obstruction to its use, this is a remarkable achievement.

29 Map of the Peak District National Park, surrounded by densely populated cities, showing the areas covered by access agreements and those to which legal access is sought.

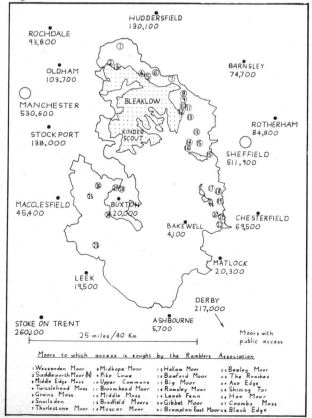

HUDDERSFIELD 130,100
ROCHDALE 93,800
BARNSLEY 74,700
OLDHAM 103,700
MANCHESTER 530,600
BLEAKLOW
ROTHERHAM 84,800
STOCKPORT 138,000
KINDER SCOUT
SHEFFIELD 511,900
MACCLESFIELD 45,400
BUXTON 20,000
CHESTERFIELD 69,500
BAKEWELL 4,100
LEEK 19,500
MATLOCK 20,300
DERBY 217,000
STOKE ON TRENT 260,100
ASHBOURNE 5,700
25 miles / 40 Km
Moors with public access

Moors to which access is sought by the Ramblers Association

1 Wessenden Moor
2 Saddleworth Moor (N)
3 Middle Edge Moss
4 Twizzlehead Moss
5 Grains Moss
6 Snailsden
7 Thurlestone Moor
8 Midhope Moor
9 Pike Lowe
10 Upper Commons
11 Broomhead Moor
12 Middle Moss
13 Bradfield Moors
14 Moscar Moor
15 Hallam Moor
16 Bamford Moor
17 Big Moor
18 Ramsley Moor
19 Leash Fenn
20 Gibbet Moor
21 Brompton East Moors
22 Beeley Moor
23 The Roaches
24 Axe Edge
25 Shining Tor
26 Hoo Moor
27 Coombs Moss
28 Black Edge

30   Friendly relations exist between farmers and the National Park wardens, as here at Wharfedale in the Yorkshire Dales National Park.

Credit for this success has been attributed to the Board's unique structure and the men and women who staff it. Undoubtedly R.N. Hutchins, the Board's Deputy Clerk for ten years, made a major contribution. But far too little credit has been given to the nominated members, especially to Phil Daley. In the early years he urged the Board to make an immediate start in securing public access to the hills and moorlands. Nor did he content himself with words! He set about the immense task of recruiting volunteer wardens from ramblers, climbers and campers who formed the core of the organised open-air movement in the urban areas surrounding the Peak. He addressed dozens of meetings in Manchester, Sheffield and Doncaster. What a response he got! Based on figures published in the Board's Annual Reports, 21,648 individual attendances from volunteers, most of them drawn from forty-six organisations, are recorded from the inauguration of the volunteer warden system until the year prior to Daley not being reappointed to the Board by Peter Walker, the Tory Minister.

Credit must also be paid to the wardens employed by the Board, which today number 13 full-time and 151 part-time wardens and assistants, plus about 200 unpaid volunteers. The wardens' dedication to the preservation of the countryside is an example which is helping to educate the millions of visitors, thereby safeguarding for posterity our most precious heritage — the uniqueness of natural beauty. What is beyond doubt, is that without the wardens the Peak's outstanding access record would never have been possible. Tom Tomlinson, who prior to his appointment as first Head Warden was for ten years warden of the Edale Youth Hostel writes:

Farmers and landowners naturally suspicious at such revolutionary thinking as National Parks and agreements for people to walk over their land, were gradually won over as the warden service became established and the wardens began to demonstrate that ramblers and climbers and people using the high moorlands were not all vandals and hooligans bent on destruction, but townsfolk who simply wanted the opportunity to walk in the countryside to breathe the fresh air and enjoy the open spaces of the great moorlands.

Nor should the financial saving, which hundreds of volunteer wardens effected, be overlooked. If only wardens on the Board's staff had been available the cost would have been many times higher than the average 9.5 per cent of total expenditure.

The acreage of access, the majority in exceedingly large stretches, has demonstrated how false were all the arguments advanced by the grouse-moor owners of the disastrous effect access would have on shooting. Bags have in no way suffered. In fact, a degree of accommodation has been developed between the ramblers and shooters which, recalling the pre-war antagonism, seemed inconceivable.

The moors have not been devastated by fires; if anything they are safer now by the presence of ramblers, but especially wardens, than ever they were in the pre-access days. Neither have the keepers been made permanent unemployables. Yet now problems of erosion have arisen, and because of the widening basis of compensation (contrary to what both Dower and Hobhouse considered were just and equitable) costs of access are increasing. Two years after the Board was established, two agreements were signed on 18 December 1953. One was with the Youth Hostels Association Trust of England and Wales for 115 acres of land including Rowland Cote Moor, Edale. The other was for nearly nine square miles, with the Duke of Devonshire on the Ashop side of the Kinder Plateau. Poetic justice indeed, for this included the area which was the scene of the famous 1932 Mass Trespass.

A celebration to mark the event was held on Good Friday 1954 in the Nag's Head pub, Edale. Alderman C.F. White, Chairman of the Peak Park Planning Board and of the Derbyshire County Council, had no doubt of its importance. He told the assembled wardens, which included 77-year-old fighter-for-access G.H.B. Ward, 'To my mind we are this Good Friday morning really opening this great National Park.' He remarked on the 'reasonably happy state of affairs between the landowners in the area and the Board.' (Sheffield Telegraph, 17 April 1954.)

The ramblers claimed that the agreement represented a great step forward in the long struggle for free access to the hills and moors.[2] It certainly did, but was by no means the end of the long contest which was to shift from the Peak to West Yorkshire, the Forest of Bowland, Snowdonia, Exmoor, Dartmoor, and may eventually reappear in the deer forests and grouse moors of Scotland.

Towards the end of 1958 negotiations were completed for access to moorland north-west of Kinder Plateau. However, before public access existed for the whole of Kinder Scout the Board had to threaten to make access orders for land on the southern approaches.[3] Fifteen owners had been involved in the negotiations for what has been described as one of the most popular walking territories in the Southern Pennines.[4]

31   Kinder Scout in winter. An access agreement to this area was signed in 1958.

In 1954 the Board decided to move into the 31 square miles of Bleaklow, an area even more remote than Kinder, with not even an undisputed public footpath;[5] the Pennine Way runs along the west edge of these moors. In December 1957 an agreement was signed with the Duke of Devonshire for access to 14½ square miles of Bleaklow.[6]

Not until the early 1960s did the Board seek to negotiate access agreements for 31 square miles of Longdendale, nearly all of which was owned by the Manchester Corporation as gathering grounds for the five nearby reservoirs. For over 100 years the Manchester Corporation had sought the rigorous exclusion of walkers from its gathering grounds so as to ensure purity of water supplies. A similar policy was pursued by other water authorities. Phil Barnes wrote in his booklet *Trespassers will be Prosecuted* that although many of these areas were publicly owned, they were 'no more accessible now than when they were in private ownership.' However necessary such an exclusion policy was in the last century, with modern filtration methods they could no longer be justified. As Tom Stephenson remarked when he, along with Phil Daley and Dr Frank Head, officials of the Manchester Area of the Ramblers' Association, discussed the problem with the chairman and officials of the Manchester Water Committee: 'I live in London and drink the water from the River Thames which before reaching my house has passed through several pairs of kidneys, yet I am still hail and hearty.' Whereas many other water authorities had installed modern plant, Manchester had refused to do so until pressure was exerted on them by the Pennine Way Campaigners. Once the new filtration and treatment works were installed access agreements were quickly signed in March 1969.

The first difficulties which confronted the Board were Windgather Rocks near Kettleshulme. These rocks were used as training grounds for young climbers. In an effort to stop the climbers the first pitches on the rock faces had been tarred, which prompted the Board to consider taking immediate action.[7] Yet in spite of the earnest and patient endeavours to negotiate access agreement no progress was made, whereupon the Board decided the best course was to purchase sufficient land at the foot of the rocks. Inability to agree upon a price resulted in the Board deciding in 1959 to make an access order for the rock face, and a strip of land below. A change of ownership, however, enabled the Board to proceed with the purchase.

The greatest difficulties were experienced with two brothers who had a sheep farm on two thousand acres of the bleakest land in the country, including the Dog Rocks at Yellow Slacks, popular with climbers, on the western edge of Bleaklow. The Peak Park authorities tried unsuccessfully to negotiate a mutually satisfactory arrangement for access. The farmers employed contractors to dynamite the rock faces, ostensibly to remove loose stone, which they said was a danger to sheep grazing. 'It is our land' one of the farmers told the *Sheffield Telegraph,* 12 February 1964, it is 'no one's business but our own, we informed the police . . . and they sent along an officer. . . . An Englishman's home is his castle, and we intend to protect ours.' Here was a prime example of the conflict between the desire for access and the right in law to the unhindered use of freehold or leasehold land.

Negotiations were eventually resolved, this time with the National Farmers' Union, with the result that the basis of compensation was considerably widened. For the first time fixed annual payments were made for the rebuilding of walls, sheep losses and the cost of extra shepherding. Where there are inadequate means of access, boundary and internal walls are damaged, and in the case of this agreement one of the most used access points was not included in the agreement.[8] As any regular country dweller knows, the greatest wall destroyers are wind, rain and frost, and above all the sheep which graze the land on many more days than the occasional visits made by either walkers or climbers.

On the top of these payments must be added wardening, which in the case of the Peak is many times more costly than compensation. The *Peak District National Park Report,* May 1975, stated that £85,376 was paid out in wardening — over 90 per cent of access costs. Now the Board is revising all earlier access agreements bringing them into line with the much heavier burden of compensation which, especially since the agreements of Bowland discussed later, have been accepted. Because of the friendly relations which exist between wardens and country lovers, wardening provides tenants, landowners and visitors with a service which gamekeepers, farmers and shepherds have never been able to offer.

The West Riding of Yorkshire The signing of access agreements on Bleaklow by the Duke of Devonshire was further evidence that on his Peak estates he had abandoned his pre-war objection to access agreements. Not so in Yorkshire, where he was still opposed to this. Following the 1949 Act the West Riding County Council had attempted to negotiate agreements in four areas covering some 13½ square miles. They included Barden Moor and

Barden Fell in Wharfedale, claimed to be the most prolific grouse moors in the British Isles and owned by the Duke. Making no progress, the West Riding County Council were considering making access orders, but quite surprisingly in July 1954 the Council informed the Government that it considered no action was necessary to secure access to the county's open country, a decision to which the Ramblers' Association objected. Much of this was grouse moors which had been the scene of many clashes between gamekeepers and ramblers since the 1930s. Tom Stephenson in a BBC discussion on 31 July 1964 stated that he had a big dossier of complaints of being hounded off the Yorkshire moors. Yet strangely enough it was the ramblers who were blamed for the decision. The County Council was negotiating for only 3 per cent of the 512 square miles of open country which existed within the West Riding boundaries; ramblers, very naturally, were asking for much more.

Some of the leading figures in the rambling movement considered that Mr Harold Macmillan, a member of the Tory Cabinet and Minister of Housing and Local Government who often shot grouse on these moors, used his influence to oppose the ramblers. This view is supported by a ministerial minute which records that he considered their proposals as 'outrageous'.[9]

Instead of proceeding to the next stage in the access machinery, the County Council proposed to provide more footpaths across the moors, claiming that these paths would serve equally well. Yet the duke's agents made extensive objections 'to the paths that have been entered on the draft maps by the Parishes covering such rambling areas as Barden Fell, Bolton Abbey moors, Pockstone and Beamsley.'[10]

The upshot of this impasse was the holding of a Public Enquiry on 26 October 1955; not only for the duke's grouse moor, but for those of other owners to which access was refused. At the conclusion of the hearing, the Inspector proposed, among other recommendations, that there should be access to Barden Moor and Barden Fell, and to some of the other moors, 'as this was the only possible course consistent with not conspiring with the West Riding County Council to circumvent the plain intentions of the Act.'[11] It was June 1957 before the Minister made known his decision, but still the West Riding procrastinated and another three years elapsed before an access agreement was finally signed in December 1960. This was followed by a further agreement in 1968, coming into operation in three stages, and lasting for 50 years, though the Council wanted it for up to 80 years. The total area covered by the agreement is 21 square miles.

No doubt the pressure from the ramblers has helped here as it did in the Peak, for between the Public Inquiry and the signing of the first agreement, there were frequent skirmishes in the area which culminated in an impressive demonstration organised by the Ramblers' Association on Yorkshire's famous Ilkley Moor. This took place in June 1958 and was attended by 2,000 people. Contingents were present from Sheffield, Manchester, Chesterfield and Liverpool in addition to many hundreds from the West Riding. The ramblers listened to speeches from the chairman of the rally urging them to trespass as it was 'the only way of showing our demands'. Lord Winster was if

32   Volunteer wardens marking the path over Barden Fell in Wharfedale, Yorkshire in 1965. This is Britain's most prolific grouse moor, and access was won after a 2,000-strong demonstration on Ilkley Moor in 1958.

anything more outspoken, urging the assembled ramblers to 'break the law, break it with a good heart and cheerful face. If you get prosecuted it will be the grandest publicity for the cause.'[12]

As the first agreement was due to expire in January 1966 the Council reopened negotiations with the Duke for a second agreement, with the intention of greatly extending the area. The Duke offered a further 1½ square miles (1,000 acres) for another five years, which in no way satisfied the Council. After much negotiation, in July 1966 they decided that unless the Duke was prepared to conclude an access agreement for the whole of Barden Moor and Barden Fell, for a period not exceeding eighty years by October 1966, they would proceed to impose an access order for the whole of the open country involved. Another two years were to elapse before the agreement was finally signed, in July 1968.

Further land became opened up as a result of the agreements signed with the Lancashire County Council and Liverpool Corporation who in addition to claiming no compensation for access to water gathering grounds signed them over in perpetuity as open to public access, though at the time they were not so popular as Barden Moor and Barden Fell.

These agreements are important, not only because they underline the value of demonstrations, but because the whole basis of compensation was being widened, going far outside what had been proposed by the Dower and Hobhouse reports that interference with property rights owing to access designation should not itself carry a right of compensation.[13] But around the time the negotiations were taking place for the second agreement, the new model clauses which increased compensation payments were being prepared. 'The principal new feature was that it made it possible for the local authorities to pay an annual consideration to the owner or tenant for what he agrees to allow or give up. . . .'[14]

The Pennine Way and Footpaths   The Pennine Way was the brainchild of Tom Stephenson, the seed being sown by two American girls who, having walked parts of the 2,000 mile Appalachian Trail in the eastern mountains of the United States of America, enquired if there was a similar walk which they could follow in England. Tom sketched out a possible route which was to form the basis of an article he wrote for the *Daily Herald* and which appeared on 22 June 1935, under the now famous caption 'Wanted! A long green trail.' Little did he know how much it really was wanted by the hill-walking public of Britain, 'who feel the call of hills and lonely places'.

It is not so lonely now! John Merrill, who completed a 2,000 miles walk in the summer of 1976, during which he walked official and unofficial long distance footpaths, reported that on the Pennine Way between fifty and seventy walkers passed him each day. Except in Snowdonia he met hardly any other walkers on his 2,000 mile journey which included the whole of the Cotswold Way, Pembrokeshire Coast Path, Cleveland Way, parts of the Two Moors Way, South West Peninsular Footpath, Sandstone Way, Peakland Way, Dales Way and Wolds Way. In fact so popular is this tough route, parts of which are not recommended for anyone who cannot steer by map or compass, that Alfred Wainwright, whose guide books to the countryside are numbered as best sellers among the walking fraternity, is considering withdrawing the offer he made in his *Pennine Way Companion*. 'If you make it have a pint on me', he said, but on 12 October 1975 he told the *Sunday Express* that it was costing him a fortune, as more than 4,000 people had claimed the free drink in four years. All types have reached the end of the Pennine Way, including blind men led by their wives.

There is no mystery surrounding its popularity. The walk along England's backbone traverses areas rich in natural beauty. Its southern end starts at Edale, a Derbyshire village which nestles under the shadow of Kinder Scout — an upland easily reached by the ramblers of the industrial north. It proceeds over Kinder Scout and Bleaklow northwards through the Brontë country of the Yorkshire Pennines, across Durham to that great Roman

33   High Cup Nick on the Pennine Way. This long distance route took thirty years to complete.

fortification Hadrian's Wall, built across the narrow neck of England, and eventually to the Cheviots and the Scottish border. Only just over one-third of its 250 miles of track needed new footpaths, yet it took thirty years to complete. The first step which set the project on its chequered way was a conference of open-air organisations held on 26 February 1938 at Hope in Derbyshire. This removed all doubts among delegates that it was either a 'press stunt, a wily move to sidetrack the access to mountains campaign or a project that would endanger the existing rights of way.'

In these early days the Pennine Way campaigners considered the Peak would present the greatest difficulties in establishing the route. Little did they know just how difficult. The conference set up a Pennine Way Association, which among others had veterans like Stephenson, Ward and Royce as members. Before World War II, helped by members of the Ramblers' Association and the Youth Hostels Association, the committee had surveyed its entire length. During the euphoria which surrounded post-war construction, plans for six hikers' highways, which included the Pennine Way, were submitted and approved by the Scott Committee and then by the Hobhouse Committee. The proposals were given legal effect by the 1949 Act following which the National Parks Commission took the project under its wings, and with slight variation approved in 1951 the route chosen in the pre-war days.

Another fourteen years were to elapse before, on 24 April 1965, 2,000 people assembled on the windswept Malham Moor and greeted with a mighty cheer the completion of Tom Stephenson's thirty-year old idea. Those thirty years were the period of greatest contention. Strangely enough some of the ramblers were not so keen, objection being taken to it crossing Kinder Scout because, to use the words of G.H.B. Ward, it may 'mar the wild character of Kinder'. He, along with others, was also concerned about the hazards which it presented to walkers unfamiliar with its changeable weather and difficult terrain. These objections were resolved at a public inquiry which accepted the proposal of a bad weather safety route.

More serious were the objections of the Manchester and Huddersfield Corporations. They claimed that walkers on the Pennine Way would increase the risk of pollution to their water supplies. While the Inspector rejected the Huddersfield claim he accepted Manchester's proposed diversion of the route for several years in the Longdendale section until Manchester had filters installed. There were other difficulties in Derbyshire which the Peak Park Planning Board resolved by purchasing the fields on the east side of Grindsbrook, which is the start of the Pennine Way. There were also problems in Northumberland. But many more long distance routes have mushroomed since these early days.

Running battles have been fought by every branch of the Ramblers' Association in an effort to retain the 100,000 miles of footpaths in England and Wales. It is estimated that up to 20 per cent are obstructed, and it is not unusual for violence to be used by landowners and farmers to prevent their use. Probably the most serious incident was the threat to use a gun in what has become known as the Battle of Bosworth Park, at Sutton Cheney in

Leicestershire, which occurred in the late 1950s. It only ended after a series of publicly advertised and well-supported walks, organised by the Ramblers' Association on Sunday 10 October 1960. In the East Riding of Yorkshire some 300 ramblers, naturalists and sympathisers walked five miles to preserve Millington Pastures, a most popular area which, under an Enclosure Award dating from 1771, was to be used only for grazing but had been ploughed up. Many farmers put bulls in fields through which paths go in an effort to deter walkers.

So serious has the threat been to footpaths in the post-war period that in May 1970 the Ramblers' Association organised a National Footpaths Week, when up to 1,000 separate events were organised in all parts of the country. Tom Stephenson describes them as perhaps the most successful venture ever organised by the Ramblers' Association.

References to Chapter 9

1 *Additional Survey Report*, Peak District National Park, July 1944, table 2. 1, p6. (The figure quoted is arrived at by totalling the three columns headed 'Moorland', 'Unimproved Grassland' and 'Scrub'.)
2 *Ramblers' News*, Winter 1953-4
3 *Peak District National Park, 15th Annual Report*, para 118
4 Ibid, *21st Annual Report*, para 49
5 Barnes, P.A., *Trespassers Will Be Prosecuted*, (1934), p20

6 *Peak District National Park, 6th Annual Report*, para 81
7 Ibid, *3rd Annual Report*, para 54
8 Rossiter, J.P., (see ref 2, Chapter 2), p201
9 Ibid, p50
10 *Ramblers' News*, Autumn 1953
11 Rossiter, J.P., *op cit*, p158
12 *Ramblers' News*, Autumn 1953
13 National Parks Committee, 1947, *op cit*, cmd 17121
14 Gibbs and Whitby, *op cit*, p32

10 Access to the Forest of Bowland

From the earliest days of the 1949 Act becoming operative, the Lancashire County Council has been urged into action by a determined force of intelligently led country lovers and users, whose endeavours could be advantageously applied to other parts of the country where similar problems exist, or are in the making. Lancashire, with 12.8 per cent of all access land, stands third to the Peak, with the Yorkshire Dales National Park second with 13.4 per cent.[1] In the early days much of Lancashire's 'open country' was outside National Parks or Areas of Outstanding Natural Beauty, and did not qualify for Exchequer grants. The ratepayer in consequence had to meet the whole of the cost, a restriction which was removed in 1968.

Barely three years after the agreement signed with the Duke of Devonshire on Kinder Scout, the Lancashire County Council signed its first agreement on 31 May 1956, which gave access to 1½ square miles of moorland. These moors are water gathering grounds, in the ownership of the Burnley Corporation. By June 1957 it extended the area by adding another 7½ square miles (4,900 acres) of Liverpool Corporation water gathering grounds. The unique feature of these agreements is the absence of any compensation, and their duration. They exist in perpetuity.

As could be quite naturally expected, other private landowners, not being representatives of the people, took a different stand. In fact so opposed were many landowners, farmers, shooting syndicates and the councils of Colne, Keighley and Trawden that they left the County Council with no alternative but to impose the first ever access order. This was for areas which included the well-known Boulsworth Hill, a ridge of rough moorland rising to 1,700 feet, situated near to the towns of Burnley, Nelson, Colne, Bradford and Halifax. There was not even a footpath over a length of four and a half miles of moorland, as they all terminated at the foot of the moor. The public inquiry held on 20 and 21 March 1956 was told that the public could gaze at Boulsworth Hill from the roads. None but the most intrepid ramblers ever roamed over its heather-clad moors. As to the danger of pollution — the objection raised by the Keighley Corporation — grouse shooters were apparently infection free; and so were picnickers who made use of an unfenced public road which crossed part of the reservoir and one of its feeder streams, to enjoy themselves on nearby land. The Inspector conducting the inquiry, though he supported the grouse shooting interests, did recommend access, because failure to do so would undermine the intention of the Act.[2] Nevertheless the Minister rejected the Inspector's recommendation, and refused to confirm either of the orders. Instead he asked the County Council to establish a footpath along the top of the hill. A vigorous altercation which the national and area secretaries had with the gamekeepers resulted in the route of the path being agreed to. However it took another twenty-two years of continuous pressure from the ramblers before a three mile long path, forty metres wide, which goes to the summit was opened. This is on land owned by the North West Water Authority. Now the ramblers are pressing the private owners over whose land the remaining seven-mile path goes, to follow the water authority's example.

Encouraged by the resistance to access from landowners and government alike, which the Lancashire County Council was experiencing south of the Ribble, some landowners in the north resorted to all the bitter hostility to access which was reminiscent of the inter-war years in the Peak. This, Tom Stephenson declared, included the largest area of moorland in England where rambling was forbidden.

34   One of the many notices still remaining on Threaphaw Fell in the Trough of Bowland.

The Forest of Bowland is no longer a forest as we understand the term today, but 310 square miles of moorland valleys in Lancashire and Yorkshire, singularly attractive to all types of country lovers, with 'varieties of scenery between the extremes of gaunt ruggedness and sylvan beauty.'[3] In the 1940s and early 1950s it was less accessible than the open country in South Lancashire, and certainly less well known than the Lake District, a few miles further north. In the Middle Ages it was reserved for the King's pleasure, as a royal hunting forest for deer and other game, and woe betide any intruder who poached the King's deer! Now the owners guarded it with equal strictness for the pleasure of the grouse shooters. For instance in August 1915 some 6,000 grouse fell victim to eight guns.

The Earl of Sefton surrounded his land with over forty 'Keep Off' and 'Private' notices, guarding it with a posse of gamekeepers and dogs. The keepers were equipped with landrovers, binoculars and loud speakers. Yet as it turned out the Earl was no more successful than his royal predecessor four centuries earlier in preserving his privacy. Of course the Earl did offer 'permit' access, but this was always outside the nesting and shooting seasons, which excluded the most desirable spring and summer months, and even then it was not unknown for a club's requests to be rejected.

Immediately following the passing of the Act, there were complaints of gamekeeper interference. Phil Barnes, Secretary of the Lancashire Branch of the Council for the Preservation of Rural England, was urging the Lancashire County Council to use the powers conferred upon the Council by Part 5 of the 1949 Act to secure legal access. They refused at that stage, accepting the landowners argument that rambling and grouse shooting were incompatible. We have already met Phil Barnes in the earlier chapters of this book. He is numbered among the outstanding Sheffield ramblers who had played a prominent part in the pre-war struggles in the Peak, being more in sympathy with the Mass Trespassers than some of his closest associates. He made a valuable contribution to the access campaign nationally, helping to prepare the Ramblers' Association memorandum which was submitted to the various immediate post-war government committees. He also appeared at Lancashire's Public Inquiries in 1956.

It was not until the early 1960s that any determined effort was made by the open-air organisations to change the attitude of the Lancashire County Council. At a 1951 conference of open-air organisations, convened by the Lancashire branch of the Council for the Preservation of Rural England, it was decided to press the County Council to seek access agreements in ten large areas of moorland south of the Ribble, access to which was fraught with the usual gamekeeper difficulties. These ten areas had been selected because of their close proximity to the large urban populations of the Manchester conurbation.

In the late 1950s access agreements had been negotiated with the Liverpool Corporation south of the Ribble. The Ramblers' Association then turned its attention to the Earl of Sefton's land. This was in response to the growing numbers of walkers who, by using cars to reach the beginning of their ramble, were able to travel further afield and in consequence were venturing upon the strictly keepered area. Learning from their earlier experiences, the organised ramblers realised how necessary it was to launch a powerful campaign if they were to succeed in gaining legal access.

Over a period many walked over the disputed area and were often challenged. Sixteen members of the Morecambe and Heysham Holiday Fellowship Rambling Club on 23 April 1960 were hailed by a loudspeaker and asked: 'Are you coming down or do we have to fetch you. We'll set the dogs on you and they'll tear you to pieces.' In another incident, a party of Fulwood Methodist Young People's Fellowship, on a ramble over the Bleasdale Fells on Good Friday 3 April 1953, were stopped by a game warden. Pupils of the Morecambe Grammar School, who were participating in the Duke of Edinburgh's Award, had a most frightening experience at the hands of a keeper, who backed up his threats by the use of physical force. This occurred on a path that was recognised as a public right of way. One of the most illuminating incidents, which illustrates the feudal atmosphere, was the treatment meted out to a parson who officiated in a neighbouring parish. He had written articles in a local newspaper describing the walks and scenery, which resulted in him being regarded as *persona non grata*, to use his own term. How very different from the days of Trollope, when it was said the 'cloth' was as keen as the gentry on the hunting field.

So strong a feeling was engendered, that Tom Stephenson in a letter to the Countryside Commission (22 January 1969) wrote: 'There was already talk of organising a mass trespass on the Abbeystead moors.' A letter addressed to Eddie Hibberd, Footpath Secretary, written on behalf of the North East Lancashire Ramblers' Association and Blackburn Co-operative Holidays Association Club, reported that 'various groups were combining to walk various routes in the area after informing appropriate bodies of their intention to do so (presumably in an attempt to arouse action which can be legally considered). Friends in Nelson, Colne, Burnley, Blackburn, Accrington and Rossendale I'm sure would give support. . . .'

Support for access extended outside the ranks of the open-air organisations. Both Fylde and Lune Valley Water Boards declared that they would not stand in the way. This powerful movement had its effect on the landowners and the County Council, though with the designation of Bowland in 1964 as an Area of Outstanding Natural Beauty a large part of the access expense involved was shifted from the ratepayer to the taxpayer.

In 1967 the Lancashire Councy Council published the report of a survey it had undertaken in 1966. One of the main conclusions of the report was that there were large areas of unenclosed moorland to which the public had no right of access. Much of this moorland consisted of fine walking country commanding panoramic views. With the growing public demand for recreational facilities in the countryside, and the proximity of these moorlands to large and expanding centres of population, it was felt that access rights for the public should be sought.

Of the 175 square miles in the Area of Natural Beauty nearly one-third were defined as open country. It was considered that the cost of securing legal access to the whole of that area would be out of all proportion to the benefits, and therefore it proposed seven areas, four of which should be given priority. These were:

1   Clougha, an area of 1,750 acres and a footpath to Ward's stone and Tarnbrook, mainly in the ownership of Lord Sefton.

2   Fair Snape/Parlick. 1,850 acres of the Bleasdale Estates.

3   Baines Crag. 90 acres belonging to Captain Gosford and Mr Hutchinson.

This totalled an area of about six square miles, though the area of open country in Lancashre was ten times larger. Assisted by the Council for the Preservation of Rural England, Colonel Houghton established unofficial contacts with the owners, and some progress was made. Yet it was not until 1969 that the Lancashre County Council opened formal negotiations. Five months earlier the Ramblers' Association decided to increase public pressure by organising a public rally in September 1969. Towards this end it set up an Action Committee, made up of representatives from the Associations of North East Lancashire, the West Riding of Yorkshire and the Lake District. It quickly gathered support from all the rambling clubs in the area, and other organisations such as the Youth Hostels Association, Friends of the Lake District and the National Trust.

As the widely based volume of support began to grow, so the landowners' attitude of uncompromising opposition gave way to one of negotiation. In fact so accommodating were they at this time, that the Lancashire County Council officials became increasingly apprehensive that the September rally would have a detrimental effect. Yet until the popular movement began to roll, the owners had been hostile.

In spite of the rain the rally held on 28 September 1969 was, in the words of the Secretary of the Ramblers' Association, Chris Hall, 'a fantastic success'. It was attended by 1,000 people, most from nearby towns but with contingents from Birmingham, Hull, the West Riding, Derby and elsewhere. The rally, held in the village of Chipping, ten miles north-east of Preston, was chaired by Arthur Raistrick, who had played such an outstanding part in the struggles in the West Riding. The rally was also addressed by Tom Stephenson, recently retired Secretary of the Ramblers' Association, who warned of possible clashes between ramblers and gamekeepers because of the increasing resentment at the continued denial of access. Though the Lancashire County Council had informed the Ramblers' Association twenty-six days prior to the Chipping rally that 'We have in fact already received agreement in principle of some of the major landowners, so much so that we hope to reach early agreement', the negotiations dragged on for another four years. The main stumbling block was the question of compensation, which was only finally settled after the Model Clauses came into effect, making it possible for an 'annual consideration' to be paid to the landowners and tenants.

Already the Chairman of the Countryside Commission had assured the landowners, writing in the *Country Landowner*, December 1969, that because of the new model access agreement, which provided for payment in advance to occupiers of land, it was 'impossible' that access orders would be made. This statement was followed up by the Director of the Countryside Commission, R.J.S. Hookway, in his address to a conference on April 14 1969, in which he was urging landowners to harvest the 'leisure crop'. He spelled out quite clearly what he meant. Payment 'should be based on consideration paid in advance, and not compensation negotiated some years after the event,' because 'the person managing the land no matter what the legal right of public access to it, needs some consideration for the fact that public access is rarely to his private interest, and more often than not to his disadvantage.'[4] Even though Mr Hookway considered this a 1970 attitude and not an 1870 one, it was contrary to the opinion of many of the access campaigners.

This was why the negotiations dragged on, even though the Action Committee, in response to the requests of the County Council, virtually suspended their campaign, persuading their members to keep off the grouse moors. In the end enough was enough; they threatened to restart the campaign, questioning the whole basis of compensation, taking their access as they wanted it, 'without any cost to the ratepayer or taxpayer', and being prepared to meet the hostility from the gamekeepers. This stopped the haggling, and the inauguration ceremony took place on Saturday 28 April 1973 to celebrate access to three of the seven areas to which the Lancashire County Council's recreational study had announced the Council's intention of seeking access. The shooting interests received £2.94 per acre in compensation, the highest amount up to that date paid for access agreements. It is interesting to note that the Lancashire County Council discovered some seven to nine months after the agreement became effective, that 40 per cent of those walking the moors were doing so before any access agreements were made.[5]

References to Chapter 10

1 Gibbs and Whitby, (see ref 9, Chapter 8), Table 2, p15
2 Rossiter, J.P., (see ref 2, Chapter 2), p145
3 Manchester and District Town Planning Committee, *Evidence Submitted to the Addison Committee* (1930)
4 Hookway, R.J.S. *Landowners and Leisure* (Countryside Commission, April 1969) pp3-4
5 Lancashire County Council, *Forest of Bowland, Area of Outstanding Natural Beauty, Recreational Survey 1973* p21

11   The Future

Achievements to Date; What of the Future?   It is nearly time to draw this account of the rise, growth and struggles of the open-air movement to a close. It has been a struggle stretching back a century and a half, to a time when the Industrial Revolution and the enclosure of common lands first forced the urban-dwelling factory and office workers to seek a renewal of fellowship, among Britain's mountains, moors and valleys. This survey has revealed that there are two facets to the pursuit of happiness. Firstly, it is unrealisable where the material essentials of life are precariously obtained. If the Industrial Revolution unlocked a new horn of plenty, it did so at tremendous human cost for the mass of the people. Through technology, it undoubtedly laid the basis for big all-round increases in living standards; but it exacted its price, not the least of which was the loss of leisure, which for some had been a marked feature of earlier societies.

As we have seen, the new techniques of industrial production, which gave rise to the industrial towns, resulted in sharpened antagonisms, which were much more acute than ever existed in earlier societies. There were those who, to escape them, longed to return to the life of earlier rural societies. For the mass of the English people there was no golden age in pre-industrial England. Others, like Rousseau, thought that happiness was only possible in solitude away from all human contact. Yet despite the powerful appeal which Robinson Crusoe wrecked on his pristine island of perfect isolation has for a people torn from their roots of a rural existence, his greatest concern was to escape back to the society of his fellow men.

So secondly, happiness cannot be realised outside the society in which we live. Nonetheless, this society has brought with it great dangers, which we ignore at our peril. In subduing a hostile environment, and through technology extracting from it its riches, we have changed it to such a degree that now, as both Shakespeare and Oscar Wilde wrote, we are in danger of killing the things we love. It is to the credit of the open-air movement that the need to preserve for posterity the bounteous gifts of nature is now better understood than at any previous time.

Before proceeding to examine the problems of the future, let me briefly summarize the practical advances of the past century and a half's struggles. Firstly, the right of legal access to mountain, moor and foreshore has been won, but it falls short of that for which the pioneers struggled, which was to wander at will, 'without let or hindrance' upon uncultivated land, and it is by no means an automatic right. To secure it requires, above all else, considerable public pressure, including, it would seem, the threat to use its most militant weapon — a situation which both Sandford and the House of Lords Select Committee on Sport and Leisure were anxious to avert. Secondly, footpaths — those ancient tracks first stamped out by animals, and the earliest means of communication — can no longer be stopped at the whim of the landowner, the farmer or developer. This is not to say this never happens! Quite the contrary; they are under constant threat of obliteration, but quite illegally so. Numbered among the greatest gains has been the provision, again not without pressure, of long distance routes; over 1,000 miles are now approved and open.

Thirdly, although National Parks are outside the scope of this study, they are very dear to the hearts and activities of all ramblers and climbers. So much of the wild country over which they roam and the crags they scale are to be found, except in Scotland, within their boundaries.

Many have noted the social distinction between those who have taken the lead in campaigning for National Parks and those who have played a similar role in the struggle for access, attributing to the former an undoubted greater success than to the latter. Though all sections of the open-air movement have campaigned for both National Parks and access, noticeable are the social distinctions between those who have formed the leading core in these respective campaigns. It has been the professional and semi-professional strata who led the National Parks movement, while on access it was the ordinary ramblers drawn from the industrial towns of the North. There are those who have attributed to these social distinctions the greater success of National Parks than of access. But this is to misread the situation. The right to walk anywhere on uncultivated land makes much greater inroads into the exclusiveness of private ownership than does the right to control the use to which private land can be put. The latter is a negative function, whereas the act of walking anywhere on uncultivated land is very positive. In any case twenty-five years experience has shown that it is the Peak National Park which has the greatest achievements to its credit. It is in this area where the struggle for access was the fiercest and most sustained, without which it is doubtful whether National Parks would ever have come into existence.

Since World War II people have had more leisure, longer holidays, a shorter working week, higher wages and more private transport, all of which have contributed to the invasion of the coast and countryside in such numbers as almost to overwhelm it. Today our National Parks are crowded with visitors and cars, so much so that the tracks are wearing out — on Kinder Scout, Ilkley Moor, and the top of Snowdon to mention only some. What will the situation be like at the end of the century when today's leisure explosion has reached nuclear proportions? By then, though population growth is slowing down, it will at a conservative estimate be around 8 per cent greater — around fifty-nine million in England and Wales. There will be demands for modern housing and extensions to existing or new towns. In the past thirty years over 17,000 square miles (eleven million acres) of land in England and Wales have been converted to urban use, at the rate of 0.1 per cent annually, and overall the area in urban use has more than doubled

35   *Experimental plastic matting being laid on the southern part of the Pennine Way near Bleaklow to combat erosion.*

since the turn of the century.[1] Private car ownership could double to some 25 million. The number of cars found in rural areas in the summer rose by 35 per cent between 1966 and 1973.[2]

Maybe because of the energy problem, the increase in car ownership will not materialise. Without a doubt other means of transport will be found, Even if the population growth is as small as projected, this will not stop greater pressure for material and cultural improvements in standards: a shorter working week covering four, or maybe three days; five or six weeks' holiday; increases in real earnings. In fact living standards could be twice as high as they are today.

Land Uses   Vital to the satisfying of all these demands is the age-old problem of land, its use, and its ownership. This has been a bone of contention for centuries, certainly since the Norman Conquest, and in a crowded island such as Britain it always will be. The varying demands for the use of land have seldom been greater, and the time is surely come when we must examine these demands in their totality, and seek a solution that will satisfy the many sided needs, irrespective of sectional interests and private gains. Within such a solution it is quite possible that the needs of the few will have to take second place to those of the majority; nor must we choose the cheapest way just because what is best in the interests of posterity is currently too expensive. Had this been the yardstick in the past some of our problems today might not have been so great.

Let me start with the need, which is too often put at the end of the queue but which has been the major concern of this study — the outdoor recreational requirements of the British people. By the end of the century the demand for recreational use of land could treble, or even quadruple, with walking, climbing (of which it is said the English are fanatics — the Countryside Commission has estimated there are 800,000 hill walkers in Great Britain), camping and nature study outstripping all other forms of leisure pursuits. The 'leisure explosion' could very well be less explosive were it probed further and appropriate action taken. As it is, ignoring this aspect of the problem, the House of Lords Committee on Sport and Leisure expected that in some areas the leisure demands on land would be so great as to exclude its use for other purposes. These other purposes are farming, the spread of urbanisation, the extractive industries, military training areas, and water. By the year 2000 the projected demand for water will be at least double today's needs. The most economical way of satisfying this demand may be by following past practice of submerging thousands of acres of valuable agricultural and recreational land, but in view of the land problems we face this is not the most sensible solution. Used water should be recycled to a much greater extent. Barrages built across coastal indentations would provide a source which could also be put to other uses, such as power production and water sports.

Since the war there has been constant pressure, supported by financial incentives, to encourage much more home produced food. New techniques have been used to transform grassland into arable land, and scrub into high quality grassland. Under the impact of mechanisation on the farm, both hedgerows and footpaths have vanished with deleterious effects on small animals, birds and humans. Where, following pressure from walkers, footpaths have been retained, it is not unknown in some cases for barbed wire reminiscent of war-time battlefields to be erected to prevent walkers straying from the track.

Of the 16 square miles of chalk downland designated as open country in Dorset 20 per cent had been ploughed by 1968 and more has now been converted. Since 1930 one-third of the North Yorkshire moors has similarly vanished. The character of about one-quarter of Exmoor National Park has been altered since 1954. Unchallenged *de facto* access has existed for years, and many who live in the area are asking, can it survive? An Exmoor Society has been formed to protect it from afforestation, and to halt the conversion of moorland vegetation into agricultural grassland. 'We intend to launch a vigorous campaign to make sure that Exmoor is conserved for the Nation', the society, told the *Western Morning News,* in July 1976. In April 1977 the Department of the Environment and the Ministry of Agriculture commissioned a report to recommend ways of ensuring a proper balance between farmers and conservationists. This — A Study of Exmoor — was delivered in November and according to *The Times,* 30 November 1977, the conservationists were delighted because it recommended 'Powers to protect moorland areas of high scenic and amenity value and to compensate farmers and landowners for any resulting loss. . . .' Unfortunately, responsibility for operating these powers is left in the hands of the existing National Park Committee which did nothing to halt the activities causing the conflict. Greater pressure than ever will therefore be needed to ensure the recommendations are carried out.

36 *Mastiles Lane in Wharfedale in the Yorkshire Dales National Park is an ancient track used centuries ago by shepherds and monks from the thirteenth century. Proposals in the 1960s to surface it for motor vehicles led to a great protest from ramblers.*

However, recreationalists and conservationists must eat, and in order to correct the imbalance of the nation's trade it is essential to produce much more of the nation's food. To discuss these and other problems affecting life in the second half of the twentieth century has deeper political implications, which neither the conservationist nor the open-air recreationalist can avoid, but which are outside the scope of this book.

An even worse picture emerges when the desecration caused by the extractive industries is considered. Every year something like 1½ square miles of land are taken for tipping and mineral waste, some of which is dangerous to health. In June 1976 the Royal Commission on Aggregates suggested Loch Etive, the Ballachulish Area, Mull and Skye, as possible sites for 'super aggregate quarries'. In the Peak, near Buxton, ICI are extending their quarrying of limestone, which is part of an area of 140 square miles. At the present rate of quarrying, the whole of the Peak's limestone mass will have been excavated to a depth of 100ft within the next eighty years. It is estimated that there are two hundred million tons of copper ore in the Snowdonia National Park which may in future be mined. For every ton of copper produced there would be 166 tons of spoil. The effect on these beautiful mountains, lakes and valleys is too horrible to contemplate if ever we permit this organised vandalism to take place. Fluorspar is essential to the production of steel, yet the major sources of supply are in the Northern Pennines and the Peak District — just those areas that are under pressure for recreational use. This is a dilemma which must be solved before future generations find that their open-air heritage has been irretrievably destroyed.

Since the middle of the last century, military departments have had powers of the most arbitrary kind for the compulsory purchase of land for the purpose of training. During World War II, as Sir Lawrence Chubb noted in an article in the Christmas 1946 issue of *Outdoors*, 'Vast areas of commons and other land — such as the South Downs, invaluable to the rambling community, were requisitioned under defence regulations.' This was a point which the Access Sub-Committee noted, when they estimated the holding in England and Wales to be in the neighbourhood of one million acres. The areas included several of immense scientific interest, outstanding for their flora and fauna and indispensable as nature reserves. Whole villages such as Tyneham in Dorset were taken over. The villagers were given a solemn pledge that they could return to their homes at the 'end of the emergency', but they have never returned. The Nugent Committee was set up to 'Examine how to reduce the demands of the Services on land, particularly in places like the National Parks and on the coast', for as Sandford noted, the Ministry of Defence have substantial holdings in three National Parks, including 145 miles of coastline in Great Britain. Yet it recommended the release of only eleven square miles out of 1,183, which is an area as big as Lancashire. Since the end of World War II, despite threats of a nuclear holocaust and the cold war there have been substantial reductions in military requirements. This has not been accompanied by a significant reduction of land used for military training. No doubt great public pressure will be needed to achieve this.

Open-Air Recreation The term open-air recreation covers many activities; rambling, climbing, water sports, bird watching, camping, fishing, and what are known as the traditional field sports — primarily hunting and game shooting. Before the 1949 National Parks and Access to the Countryside Act made it possible for the public in England and Wales to walk legally over private land which had been almost exclusively used for the traditional field sports, a degree of multiple use had been forced on the owners of some of these areas by the rambling fraternity. This is known as *de facto* access, or access by sufferance, and for a number of reasons it still exists to a far greater extent in Scotland than in the Peak District. In a country with a high population density, the multiple use of land is of the utmost importance. So far as the ramblers, and to a lesser extent the climbers, are concerned, I have traced the history of the conflicts which have compelled the need for access to be recognised as an element of growing importance in its multiple use. The problem for the future is, how can the rapidly growing demand for future recreational needs be adequately met alongside all other essential needs? Yet before going on to discuss this, let me examine the purposes which today lie behind the provision of such facilities.

As we may have seen, many men and women go out into the country to escape as a relaxation from their work and life in the industrial towns. They not only want to see a landscape pleasing to the eye, in contrast to the ugly towns, they feel the urge to walk over difficult terrain, climb mountains, scale crags in co-operation with their fellows. Today this spirit probably burns stronger in the breast of the rock climber and mountaineer than in any other section of outdoor enthusiasts, and this is probably one of the reasons why it is estimated that there are 50,000 climbers in Britain today, most of them young. To strengthen this moral purpose should be the motivation behind the measures that are taken to meet the leisure explosion. Yet the impression left by the statements of those charged with providing the facilities is one of manipulation. The diversion of the millions of country visitors into forms of gregarious passive activities provides something akin to the popular seaside resorts, but with trees and valleys, instead of the bands, crowds and shows.

It is correct to say that there is not a total lack of concern with providing for the upland rambler and climber. After fifty years of struggle how could there be? Nonetheless, there is an extreme reluctance to disturb the *status quo*, and this is only done when there is a threat of confrontation. It is only fair to say that this is a reflection of government policy. As we have already seen, Circular 96 issued to Local Authorities and giving advice on how to apply the 1949 Act, urged that 'friendly understanding or mutual indifference between landowners and ramblers should not be disturbed'.

The first question that arises is: is there the land available to provide for the needs of the upland rambler and climber? The Institute of Terrestial Ecology in 1976 claimed that approximately one-third of Britain's total land is mountainous, ie above 800 feet. The House of Lords Select Committee on Sport and Leisure spelled out the problem more precisely when it pointed out that a large part of the population live at one end of our island and most of the open access country is at the other. In South-East England, where population density is highest, high land prices and intensive lowland farming combine to make public access to the countryside difficult; Scotland, which has one-third of the whole land area of Britain, has only one-tenth of the population, with 95 per cent of that area being occupied by only 10 per cent of those people. Responsibility for this situation rests solely on successive governments, whose policies, starting with the Highland Clearances, have resulted in de-populating the glens, making them the playground of the wealthy, and not only of English but of foreign tourists as well. Half the clients of the Scottish grouse moors are rich French, Germans and Americans. There are those who want to keep it this way. Yet even in Scotland, with its vast expanses of open country, social and leisure problems are developing. Tourists attracted by the vast expanses of natural beauty have gone there in numbers, producing on a smaller scale many of the problems now commonplace in parts of England and Wales.

The 1949 Act was designed to meet the needs of the preservationists and the rambler. Many consider the most important provision of the 1968 Act was the power given to Local Authorities to provide Country Parks. It also broadened the scope of access arrangements by extending open country to include woodlands, rivers or canals. It extended the area eligible for grant aid. Ploughed up footpaths had to be restored not later than six weeks from the date of giving notice of the intention to plough. It also granted to the Minister power to make an order in respect of land in a National Park which is predominantly moor or heath. Where an order is made the occupier may not plough moor or heath, which has not been agricultural land in the preceding twenty years without giving six months written notice to the Local Authority.

However not everyone was very enthusiastic about the Act. Mr W.S. Tysoe, elected President of the Ramblers' Association in 1978, wrote in *Rucksack* for January 1969: 'While much of the Countryside Act was welcome, there were those of us who suspected its emphasis on "using" the countryside as against the preserving of natural beauty. . . . Those of us who felt critical pointed out that no clear idea had been given of what activities would be catered for in the Country Parks. . . .' I would go further and suggest, based on the statements of the Chairman of the Countryside Commission to the House of Lords Select Committee on Sport and Leisure, that the purpose of these parks is to manipulate the millions now seeking enjoyment in the countryside. He said 'The management of people in ways we hope will not be too noticeable to them are general questions which are looming very large.' Mr John Cripps explained that this was to be achieved by the provision of Country Parks and picnic sites, in order 'to intercept people between the towns where they live and the National Park to which they might otherwise go'.[3]

The Commission is concerned with access. Nonetheless they are not anxious to disturb *de facto* access unless there is a danger of confrontation. Access so far as the Commission is concerned, is largely a question of providing long distance footpaths and bridleways.[4] Yet according to John Newham, Field Officer of the Ramblers' Association, the Commission's interest in long distance paths is waning, following their rejection of proposals to develop the long distance paths net-work.

When the facilities provided are examined, it is clear that they follow the pattern as outlined by Mr Cripps. There are now 116 Country Parks, 153 picnic areas, thirteen long distance footpaths and bridleways (Countryside Commission 1974-5 Report), but what of access? Based on the information set out in Gibb's and Whitby's study *Local Authority Expenditure on Access Land*, there was up to 1 April 1973, 135 square miles of land to which the public have legal access. There are no precise figures available as to the extent of open country; the nearest obtainable is 170,000 square miles of rough grazing of little value for agriculture. Thus twenty-eight years after, under the 1949 Act only 1.9 per cent of open country is legally accessible. 82 per cent of all access land, and much of the *de facto* access land, is in northern England, within reasonable travelling time of the great Lancashire and Yorkshire conurbations, while 56 per cent of it is in the Peak, which as Rossiter, Gibbs and Whitby point out has dominated the pattern of growth. The areas which are now in the greatest need have a pitifully small amount of access land, and the *de facto* land is vanishing at an alarming rate with footpaths which are also in danger from so-called 'rationalization'.

The Countryside Commission with its policies of shepherding people away from the wild parts of Britain, is undermining the spirit of adventure, which has been an essential part of the human race since the beginning of time. One of the reasons for this is the refusal to face up to the controversial issue of the desire to roam freely over all uncultivated land. In place of this has been substituted the piecemeal approach, which in twenty-eight years since its introduction has allowed landowners, aided and abetted by some Local Authorities and unsympathetic governments, to take maximum advantage of delaying procedures to hold up progress.

It is also necessary to draw attention to the Criminal Law Act 1977. The Ramblers' Association are concerned that it may be used against ramblers, but the Department of the Environment have given assurance that the Act is directed against those who try by force to enter premises and property, and it is not intended for use against ramblers. This is undoubtedly true, yet neither were the Acts relating to trespass and to poaching, which have often been used to restrain ramblers walking on uncultivated moorlands.

Plans for the Future   By the time this appears in print, all access plans from the National Parks should be known. At the time of writing only the draft plans exist. It is pertinent to start with Scotland, for though it is outside the arrangements for England and Wales, it is the part of the country where at the end of the last century the fight for access originated and, paradoxically, the place where least has been achieved.

It is fashionable these days for everybody concerned with securing legal access to mountain and moor, to pay lip service to James Bryce. Unfortunately many lack his courage and understanding as to what are the obstacles which hold up restoring the freedom to roam. Even more important they ignore the lessons to be drawn from the struggle of the last three-quarters of a century. In no part of Great Britain are both these points more pertinent than in Scotland, where private land ownership on a large scale is probably more extensive than in any other part of Great Britain. 140 individuals or companies own just over half the Highlands and Islands; four individuals own nearly half a million acres (*The Times*, 29 March 1976). Scotland is no longer solely the playground of the Royalty and wealthy sportsmen. Over two million people visit it each year. The vast majority to enjoy its beauty without killing its wild life, and though the Red Deer Commission have claimed there is no need for conflict between hill walking and deer stalking, recent experiences seem to belie this claim.

Catering for the grouse shooting and deer stalking requirements of visitors is now big business in Scotland, with hunters coming from most countries in Europe as well as America and Canada. To provide for the leisure explosion the Scottish Recreational Association was formed in September 1972 'to serve, unite and represent' all those concerned with the management of recreational amenity and with its impact on the more traditional land uses.[5] But before the non-shooting recreationalist rushes off in even greater numbers to sample the facilities offered, let them examine precisely what is the fare.

First of all the Scottish landowners have never been keen on National Parks, and most emphatically not of the American type. They are quite enthusiastic for Country Parks because 'A Country Park is a limited area of land, usually about 200 acres, which retains its rural aspect, but where recreational requirements take precedence over farming and forestry. The area invariably will be managed by a Local Authority. Within the Park, facilities will be provided to attract and hold the visitor; these will vary, but will certainly include car parks, lavatories, information points and picnic sites. There may also be more elaborate installations, such as paddling pools, a water-ski centre, nature trails and games pitches. *The object of the country park is to act as a sponge to absorb as large a number of visitors as possible in attractive surroundings, and thus take the pressure off other vulnerable areas.*'[6] Nor are the sporting-estate owners opposed to access agreements: 'properly managed public access, while providing a new source of highly acceptable revenue, *can be a sensible and civilised way to divert pressure from the more vulnerable areas. . .*'[7] In fact so keen are they for such agreements that they have chided the Local Authorities for 'not accepting their responsibilities in this line'.[8]

What sort of access agreements do the landowners want? Certainly not the extensive type of agreements with the minimum of restriction, such as exist in the Peak, nor even the much smaller sized agreements as were negotiated in Bowland, with *de facto* access on most of the surrounding grouse moors. What they are seeking are small enclaves within the wider expanses, to which 'Access is technically illegal' which would mean the end of all sufferance access. Efforts to negotiate one such agreement were made over a number of years and finally broke down, because Colonel Grant in the Rothiemurchus area of the Cairngorms — one of Britain's most sought after mountainous recreational areas where *de facto* access already exists — wanted restriction on access during the deer stalking season written into the agreements. On top of this, he wanted restrictions in May and June for the sake of the grouse.[9] What is more the landowners urged the appointment of wardens by the Local Authority 'for enforcing any necessary regulations'.[10] This would certainly include preventing the public spilling over onto neighbouring land where such contracts will not operate.[11]

Why should the bulk of Scotland's two million tourists be held in sponge like countryside parks, or policed in narrow access areas just to provide the owners of Scotland's sporting estates with bigger profits? It has proved impossible to discover the number of stalkers and shooters visiting Scotland each year. It is unlikely to exceed more than 20,000, and yet the land

37   Rothiemurchus in the Cairngorms, Scotland, where access negotiations broke down because the owner wanted no access during the grouse nesting and deer stalking seasons, May to October.

required to rear a quarter of a million deer and many more grouse and other game birds is around two-and-half million acres, or thirteen per cent of the land area of Scotland. Which leaves the remaining visitors, many of whom are as eager to sample Scotland's solitude as the traditional sportsmen, with what is left.

Faced with this situation what has the Countryside Commission for Scotland done? When they were launched in 1967 and made responsible for 98 per cent of the area, they wrote how encouraged they were '. . . by the wealth of goodwill shown by the representatives of the land owning, farming and forest interest'. Before those words were ever written the Scottish Land Owners' Federation had, in their publication, already started to make clear their attitudes to access and National Parks. So it is not surprising that within the next five years the efforts made to negotiate an access agreement covering a fairly wide expanse in the Rothiemurchus area of the Cairngorms broke down.

It would be unfair to state that the Commission has totally failed in its most important duty. It has secured some access but in the main they are 'linear' agreements which, according to the Director of the Countryside Commission, in Scotland 'Can vary in width from a few feet of footpath in some situations to as much as sixty yards wide in others.'

According to the statement of Mr Prior (Secretary of the Countryside Commission for Scotland) to the Access to the Countryside Conference held on the 4 December 1975, 'Negotiations are now in progress or are being contemplated in more than twenty cases to our knowledge, including extensive areas of mountain and moorland.'[12] However, the Director of the Scottish Countryside Commission is not prepared to identify these areas because 'Negotiation for an interest in land is a delicate business and the less publicity given to it until the parties are in agreement the better', (letter dated 2 March 1977). This is quite contrary to experience in the Peak, on Barden Moor and Barden Fell and on Bowland, where but for the public pressure from the ramblers, no agreement would have been reached.

The National Trust for Scotland had no such inhibitions when they sought to negotiate agreements covering its Highland properties including Killiecrankie, Linn of Tunnell and Craigower in Perthshire. Unfortunately the negotiations have fallen through, but not because of any deer stalking problems, for the Trust does not let stalking on its mountainous property. The reason is that agreement could not be reached on the amount of compensation, which the Trust maintains would not cover '. . . the cost of providing for the services for the future when they have access to our land', (letter dated 23 December 1977).

Two other matters need touching on before leaving backward Scotland. The first one is what Mr Prior describes as the 'mythology' that there is no Law of Trespass in Scotland. This is 'trotted out', as he put it, 'whenever a suitable opportunity arises.' These occasions invariably arise whenever the need for legal access is discussed. Always it is claimed that there has in the past been a greater degree of sufferance access in Scotland than in England. This is because of the much smaller urban population and its remoteness from the more extensive areas of cultivated land, with the result that the prolonged confrontations such as were experienced in the Peak and West Yorkshire have never occurred in Scotland. Now this is changing and it is time that the true measures of the problem was grasped.

The other issue is that of National Parks. Scotland, next to the Lake District has figured prominently in the campaigns for National Parks. In Scotland, owing mainly to the private landowners' hostility, there are no National Parks whatsoever, and the Countryside Commission for Scotland has dropped the idea. To replace them they are proposing Regional and Special Parks, which it is claimed are more appropriate to Scotland. They believe that the Scottish Land Owners Federation are in general support of these proposals. After reading the Federation's response to them and bearing in mind the whole sorry history of National Parks and access in Scotland I am far from sure. To discuss it in detail would go outside the scope of this book. I hope others will quickly take it up, otherwise the National Park concept as applied to Scotland will continue to remain a visionary's dream.

It is some relief to turn from the disappointing Scottish scene to England

and Wales. Outside of the Peak District, however, there is little to be pleased about. Even in the Peak there is cause for concern. So far as I can discover no authority has any specific plans for any extension of area-wide access land, even though serious access problems are arising. Typical is the statement in the Yorkshire Dales draft plans: 'The ever increasing pressure of recreational use is however creating problems . . . because access to traditional areas is being restricted or because of the general inadequacy of existing provisions.' What do they plan to do? 'Extend or safeguard existing public access by selective application of formal access agreement.' A very general statement with no specific proposals. The North Yorkshire Moors National Park authority is more forthright. While admitting that there are problems they are '. . . not trying to increase access to open land. . . .' A similar position exists in the Northumberland National Park.

In Snowdonia, a very popular area, there are fairly acute problems, brought about by what has been described as the mass invasion of hill walkers and climbers. Some farmers have even tried to prevent walkers going into the mountains, but they have failed! Eight years ago the Welsh Office purchased

38 Snowdonia, where although invaded by walkers and climbers, there is still no legal access.

the mountain section of Snowdonia, but they were subsequently pressed by the tenant farmers to re-sell the land to them. To this the Secretary of State agreed providing they would sign irrevocable access agreements. Very shortly it is expected that the first such agreement will be signed, though both climbers and walkers would prefer the land to be retained by some public authority. Shortly after the purchase, the Ramblers' Association was approached by the Park Planning Authority to dissuade their members from venturing on the Nantlle Hills in order not to prejudice 'delicate negotiations'. The request was acceded to but nothing has been gained. Now the Merseyside and North Wales Area of the Ramblers' Association supported by the Committee for Wales of the British Mountaineering Council have decided '. . . to claim the freedom of the hills in the Nantlle district of Snowdonia'. They held their first official ramble in the area in September 1977.

The Lancashire County Council, which is the Authority responsible for land in the Trough of Bowland and Boulsworth Hill areas, is unable to state what its 'plans will be with respect to the future of access areas', (letter dated 21 March 1977).

The Exmoor National Parks Committee Draft Plan contained no proposals for extending legal access. In fact the only open country which is entirely safe is the 17 square miles in the ownership of either the National Trust or the National Park Committee, as the President of the Ramblers' Association told its National Council meeting in April 1977.

39   There are still no plans for legal access to Exmoor.

The situation in the Peak is somewhat better. Its outstanding access record is well known, though it must be pointed out that following the access arrangements for North Longdendale and Shelf Moor, totalling 17 square miles and concluded in 1956, only 3 square miles of access land has so far been negotiated. The last was the purchase of land for the well-known climbing area of Stanage Edge in 1971. It may of course be considered that there is little need for more access land in the Peak, but this is not so. The number of visitors to the area is increasing every year and more are coming to walk over its famous moors and climb the many crags, which is causing serious problem of erosion. This is why it is so essential to extend access to more uplands, moorlands and rock outcrops.

The Peak's plans for the future are quite specific in contrast to the generalized plans of the other Park Authorities. Regarding the northern area of the Peak — which is described as 'wild moorland country' noted for its 'remoteness from human influence' — a pledge is given that 'Existing access agreements will be maintained and negotiations for new agreements continued or entered into. . . .' No such specific undertaking is given for the eastern or south-west moors. Here access agreements *may* follow from studies being made. Nevertheless pressure on these areas is quite heavy, particularly the Staffordshire Roaches and the moorlands near Sheffield.

The most worrying proposal to appear in the Peak District National Park Plan for 1978 is the possibility that in addition to the exclusion of the public during the twelve days of the shooting season new access agreements may contain restrictions for the purposes of 'nature conservation', in particular to the heather moors, to which the report admits the owners are reluctant to allow public access because these are '. . . the most valuable grouse moors . . . few of which are currently subject to existing access agreements'.[13] There are two proposed restrictions for limiting access. The first during the Springtime nesting season; the second to 'defined paths'. Justification for these drastic restrictions is to protect wild life, especially birds of prey. The only evidence offered is the '. . . very strongly expressed views from naturalists that free access can inhibit the more sensitive nesting birds. . . .'[14] Until a scientific investigation can establish the real cause, Sheffield ramblers are refusing to accept these new restrictions and have asked the Board to negotiate immediate unrestricted access to twenty-eight moorlands which will help to relieve the growing pressure on such well-known uplands as Kinder Scout and Bleaklow.

The Peak is also the most important climbing area in Britain, with some seventy rock faces, over half of which are of national importance. The eastern side of the upper Derwent valley is an area in which there is the most continuous series of gritstone edges to be found in England. There are some tens of thousands of climbers living within easy reach of this area. While the Peak District National Park has done much to assist the climbers, there still remain a few problem areas such as Tintwistle Knarr and the limestone dales.

In no sense are these comments intended to be a review of all the draft plans of the ten National Parks. I have only touched on those areas which are subject to the greatest pressures. Even if all the Parks had the specific plans of the

Peak, there still remain obstacles which will have to be overcome before the freedom to roam on all of Britain's wild uncultivated land is realised. The most important are the financial constraints imposed by the Government, and the increasing '. . . cost involved in making compensatory payments to land owners and wardening the areas', (letter from the Lancashire County Council 21 March 1977). Rossiter, and also Gibbs and Whitby, have investigated these factors. The compensation per acre is rapidly increasing, going far beyond what both Dower and Hobhouse ever envisaged. While figures quoted by Rossiter and Gibbs and Whitby are not strictly comparable, they do give a rough guide as to trends. The greatest percentage of expenditure is the cost of wardening and compensation. The first point to note is that whereas in the early access agreements costs of wardening far exceeded other factors, according to Gibbs and Whitby wardening costs in spite of inflation are rapidly declining. In 1973/4 the cost of wardening was 52 per cent of total expenditure[15], declining to 32.4 per cent in new access areas[16]; whereas the cost of compensation is very much in the opposite direction — 26 per cent in 1973/4[17] increasing to 69.5 per cent in new access areas.[18] Quite an alarming trend!

Whereas the majority of acquisitions were on lowland sites, it is interesting to note the attempt by the Peak District National Park to purchase parts of Kinder Scout in 1976, and also the action forced on the Secretary of State for Wales who, because of the failure to conclude access agreements on Snowdon, has purchased the massif. It must however be pointed out that wardening costs for upland sites are one-fifth lower than for lowland sites. Therefore ramblers and climbers should not be put off in applying pressure for access agreements in upland areas because the National Park Authority puts forward this argument.

The reasons for this are clear. Firstly, private owners of land needed for access have increasingly extracted more money from Local Authorities and secondly, despite the Local Authorities' reluctance to acquire the land, this has been forced upon them by the private owners who, aware of the increasing number of visitors, particularly to the most accessible land, prefer to sell rather than make access agreements. Over half of the arrangements for access in 1974/5 were through public acquisition whereas in 1956/7 it was nil.[19]

References to Chapter 11

1 Department of the Environment, *The Countryside: Problems and Policies* (Discussion paper), para 33
2 Ibid, para 27
3 House of Lords, (see ref 9, Chapter 8), para 80, p25
4 Ibid, para 80, p26
5 *Scottish Field Sports Report*, 1973, p15
6 Scottish Landowners' Federation, *Landowning in Scotland*, No 143, April 1971, (my emphases)
7 *Scottish Field Sports Report*, 1973, p15 (my emphases)
8 House of Lords, *op cit*, para 1407, p409
9 *Rucksack*, Autumn 1973

10 Scottish Landowners' Federation, *Access Without Tears*

11 Countryside Commission for Scotland, *Fifth Annual Report,* p27

12 *Conference Report,* Access to the Countryside Conference 1975, p18

13 Peak District National Park, *National Park Plan,* 1978, para 7.21, p65

14 Letter to the Secretary of the Ramblers' Association, South Yorkshire and North-East Derbyshire Area, 20 Dec 1977

15 Gibbs and Whitby, (see ref 9, Chapter 8), table 8, p22

16 Ibid, table 28, p69

17 Ibid, table 8, p22

18 Ibid, table 28, p69

19 Ibid, figure 1, p11

12   *What Needs to be Done*

The words 'rambling craze' have been used to describe the big expansion of rambling in the 1930s, with 10,000 people going into Derbyshire every weekend. Thirty years on, the term 'leisure explosion' is employed to illustrate an even greater expansion: *Mountain Life* for October/November 1975, claims that over one million people are involved in mountain activities. The problem now is, how can it be stopped from becoming, by the end of the century, the Armageddon between land users and leisure?

Since 1948 the amount of land for which agreements for public access have been negotiated is pitifully small. Its planned increase is no greater than in the past. In some areas where the need is rapidly growing, it is virtually non-existent. Through farming and other uses, where the need is greatest, the designation 'open country' has been changed, and access by 'sufferance' which is always a precondition for legal access, has been automatically extinguished.

Under the pressure of the countryside invasion, and in an effort to contain it, Country Parks and picnic sites have been provided, and are appreciated by many who visit them. Yet the user of these facilities today will be the upland walker and climber of tomorrow, none more so than our young people. The provision of nature trails and long distance footpaths is evidence of this. Far from satisfying the urge to roam at will over large stretches of the most alluring moors and scrub lands, they merely whet the appetite. So they should, but for them to play their part in introducing the people to the uplands, the Countryside Commission's approach needs a change of emphasis. Visitors need encouragement to wander beyond the confines of Country Parks.

Out of these deliberations should emerge a plan of future land needs for the remaining years of this century. The question naturally arises, are the present methods of dealing with these problems adequate? So far as the upland walker and climber is concerned, the answer is no. Access has been granted where the conflicts have been the greatest. If they are to be avoided in future, then it is essential to anticipate further needs. The study of Gibbs and Whitby has already pointed out that public acquisition of land is increasingly being forced on the Authorities as the vehicle for public access. Why not ignore all the doctrinaire arguments, and face the reality of the trends — which have emerged on an increasing scale since 1957 — and replace access agreements, which are subject to periodic re-negotiation and increasing cost, by publicly acquiring all the land required for outdoor recreational activity?

Those who raise cost as an objection must face the fact that it is the public acquisition of land needed for access which is a main factor in the rising cost of access land. Furthermore, surely it is worth while spending money to avoid social conflict, especially when, however the issue is tackled, the end result is likely to be the same. For just as the northern rambler in the first forty years of the century refused to be excluded from the grouse moors of the Peak, so will the ramblers and climbers of the future refuse to be excluded from Exmoor, Dartmoor, and the deer forests and grouse moors of Scotland. The choice is clear, either an orderly civilized process of obtaining access, or conflict.

Experience shows that where there is no exclusive private ownership of land, there is much greater tolerance between users. Now with the danger of pollution removed, there are few conflicts between walkers and water authorities on their water-gathering grounds. The Forestry Commission, Britain's largest landowner, claims that 'once a forest becomes reasonably mature we provide access as a matter of policy, and if a choice has to be made between the shooter on the one hand, and the camper and rambler on the other, they give priority to the latter'. Even so ramblers regret the loss of *de facto* access which they took before it was planted.

There has never been any access problem on land held by the National Trust. On some common land, where user rights are shared, there have been few access problems. Since their inception, the National Parks of America are publicly owned and managed — they cover about 11 million acres or 1 per cent of all US area . . . to which the public has permanent access.[1] The President of the Ramblers' Association told the National Council at its meeting in April 1977 that not all American National Parks were acquired when the country was uninhabited and uncultivated. 'When attempts were first made at the turn of the century to establish a National Park in the Great Smoky Mountains on the borders of Tennessee and North Carolina, the area was completely controlled by private owners . . .' — and there were no less than 6,600 separate tracts.

Already the Scottish Labour Party has called for the nationalisation of all sporting estates in Scotland. The National Council of the Ramblers' Association in 1973 called for the public or quasi-public ownership of a greater proportion of land in the National Parks, which was supported later by the minority report to the Sandford Committee. Even the Government itself has urged '. . . A more vigorous policy of public acquisition.'

It is significant among outdoor recreationalists how this demand is coming to the fore again. Commenting on the correspondence which the Battle of the Spey provoked, the editor of *Mountain Life* drew attention to the proposal for land nationalisation which he claimed was in the Scottish Nationalist Party manifesto. He attacked what he described as the 'moral position' where 'in the Highlands of Scotland, less than 300 families own more than five million acres of land.' The Editor drew attention to the Free Air Act in Norway, which allows free access to uncultivated land.[2]

The main burden of campaigning for these demands obviously falls on the shoulders of all open-air organisations. There are more of them today and their combined membership is greater than ever before. Varying estimates

40   Queueing up to climb on the Idwal Slabs in Snowdonia.

have been made of the size of the ramblers' organisations. During the 1930s Tom Stephenson, with many years' active association with the rambling movement, estimated its membership in that period as between 35,000 and 40,000, and the number of clubs affiliated at between 300 and 400.[3] The Youth Hostels Association was started in 1929, and grew rapidly in the 1930s; by September 1933 its membership numbered 28,000.[4] Today the Ramblers' Association has a recorded membership of 30,000; the Youth Hostels Association is many times larger, with a record figure of 277,526, a 13 per cent increase over the previous year. The Camping Club has 122,500 members and the climbers have a membership of around 50,000 organised in 200 clubs.

It is now the time for the open-air organisations to draw closer together. Were they to act in unison with a massive public campaign, such as happened in the 1930s, the impact would be enormous.

Looking back over the long years of struggle for access, it is noticeable that the greatest support for the campaign has come from those on the left of the broad political spectrum, rather than from those on the right. It was the radical Whigs of the eighteenth century who were prominent in the struggle to retain London's commons. Many of the early founders of the rambling clubs, notably G.H.B. Ward, were dedicated socialists. Throughout its chequered parliamentary career many of those who sponsored Private Bills were Labour MPs. The three Bills which in the post-war period have reached the Statute Book were all Labour Government measures. In the application of the Acts, Labour Local Authorities have on the whole been more willing to administer them.

A noticeable weakness has been the reluctance of the open-air organisations to make determined efforts to secure greater support for their policies from the broad labour movement; particularly so the Trades Union Congress, without doubt the most influential body in Britain today, whose interests are beginning to spread beyond work and wages to the social problems such as education and health.

One lesson which shines like a beacon through all the long years of struggle for access is the vital importance of public demonstration. It was this which saved the London Commons; over a period of forty years it won many notable victories in the Peak, secured access to Barden Moor in West Yorkshire, and partial access to Bowland in Lancashire. Drawing upon the lessons of the past it is within our power to make the dreams of James Bryce, G.H.B. Ward, Edwin Royce and Tom Stephenson become a living reality.

References to Chapter 12

1 *The Great Outdoors of the USA*, (US Department of Commerce and United States Travel Service Brochure), 1943
2 *Mountain Life*, No 18, February-March 1975, p27
3 Rickwood, P.W., (see ref 5, Chapter 6), p189
4 Joad, C.E.M., *A Charter for Ramblers*, (London, nd), p17

Acknowledgements

My thanks are due to many people too numerous to mention, officials and members of open air organisations who have given their time in recalling memories of incidents in which they were involved while trying to win access to mountains. They also loaned me photographs.

In particular mention must be made of Tom Stephenson, for many years secretary of the Ramblers' Association, and Bernard Rothman, who led the Kinder mass trespass.

Many read the first draft and made helpful suggestions, most of which have been included in the final text. Special thanks are due to Professor John Saville and David Rubinstein who helped me to concentrate the story on the essentials. However, responsibility for the text and judgements are mine.

I am indebted to the staff of the Sheffield Central Library for making available all their material and obtaining all I requested from other sources. I would also like to thank the typist, Jos Kingston, and my wife Mary for their many helpful suggestions which have improved the text.

Grateful acknowledgements are due to the following for use of illustrations: B. Andrews: 34; J. Bantoff: 11, 28; D.J. Bennet: 19, 37; D. Berwick: 24, 31; J.A. Brimble, ARPS: 1; G.L. Carlisle: 13; H. Hill: 20, 22, 25, 26; The Holiday Fellowship Ltd: 4, 5; Manchester Public Libraries: 16; D. Mayes (Plas Y Brenin National Centre for Mountain Activities): 40; M. McKay: 29; Peak Park Planning Board: 35; The Ramblers' Association: 2, 12, 17, 33, 38, 39; The Ramblers' Association (Manchester Area): 6, 18, 21, 27; F. Rodgers: 14; Sheffield City Libraries: 23; C.R. Stevens: 3; B. Unne: 32; Miss F.E. Ward: 7, 9, 10; Yorkshire Dales National Park: 30, 36.

Index